PRAISE FOR *CONSORTING WITH SPIRITS:*

"Miller has written the definitive, next-level book on working with spirits. This is not for beginners, yet he takes many complicated texts and breaks them down into relatable exercises for the 21st-century magic worker. No matter your level of experience, if you work with spirits in any manner, you will find a gem of wisdom in *Consorting with Spirits*."

—Jacki Smith, author of *Coventry Magic with Candles, Oils, and Herbs*, and *The Big Book of Candle Magic*, founder, Coventry Creations

"This latest offering from Jason Miller fills a gap in the literature of occultism that we didn't know we had. It's a plain-spoken, anecdotal guide to spirit communication. But don't let the breezy approach fool you into thinking it's another pop occult book. It reminds me of Jess Stearn's *Yoga, Youth, and Reincarnation* in its mix of personal experience with references to the serious—and seriously intimidating—genre of ceremonial magic and what Miller calls 'Sorcery.' For many people who are thinking of dipping their toe into the subject by getting practical experience, Miller's guide is a perfect (and non-denominational) companion. For those who have been studying the more academically-oriented tomes on magic, and become more bewildered by the hour in the mix of dead languages and dead wizards, this will clear up some of the confusion. Miller has the background and is generous with sharing his own experiences, and for that reason alone the book is worth the price of admission."

—Peter Levenda, coauthor of *Rites of the Mummy*

"Jason Miller has written an engaging and highly useful guide to spirit work. Smart, funny, and, most importantly, practical, this is a book rooted in historical methods of magic but not bound by them. I especially liked how Jason looks at the various approaches to the spirits from multiple lenses: Christian, Pagan, and Luciferian with a bit of Tibetan Buddhism thrown in for good measure. Top notch."

—Aidan Wachter, author of *Weaving Fate*

"Witty, insightful, engaging, enjoyable, and a definite game changer. *Consorting with Spirits* is everything you would expect from Jason Miller and more!"

—Christopher Ora
and cc

"For many witches, sorcerers, magicians, and the like, working with an assortment of spirits is central to their practice. Spirit work is certainly one of the cornerstones of my practice. Jason Miller's *Consorting with Spirits* is a rare treasure. This book manages to provide a sensible frame of reference for spirits, a balanced mix of level-headed caution with confidence-building encouragement, and a rational discussion of practical techniques. This book is for people who actually want to work with spirits, not just think about them. The personal experiences and insights Jason shares are gold for those who are ready to improve their practice. I am heartily recommending this book to all my students."

—Ivo Dominguez Jr., author of *The Four Elements of the Wise*

"At long last—modern witchcraft has been provided what it so very much needs: a clear and concise guide to actually advancing your practice. Jason Miller's *Consorting with Spirits* is an affably frank and detailed look at how any practitioner may go about forging connections with a variety of different types of spirits without getting their butt kicked. This will be an invaluable book to any witch wanting to progress beyond 101."

—Tara-Love Maguire, coauthor of *Besom, Stang & Sword*

"Excellent, practical techniques for experienced occultists interested in expanding their practice to include working with spirits. Thoughtful and insightful, there's much to learn, ranging from working with well-known spirits to ancestors to local spirits with lots of exciting magic to add to your witchcraft. One of my new favorite books!"

—Deborah Castellano, author of *Magic for Troubled Times* and *Glamour Magic*

Consorting
with Spirits

Consorting
with Spirits

Your Guide to Working with Invisible Allies

JASON MILLER

Foreword by Mat Auryn

WEISER BOOKS

This edition first published in 2022 by Weiser Books, an imprint of
Red Wheel/Weiser, LLC

With offices at:
65 Parker Street, Suite 7
Newburyport, MA 01950
www.redwheelweiser.com

ISBN: 978-1-57863-754-6

Library of Congress Cataloging-in-Publication Data available upon request.

Cover art © Wojciech Zwoliński/Cambion Art
Interior by Debby Dutton
Typeset in Weiss Std and Lato

Printed in the United States of America
IBI
10 9 8 7 6 5 4 3 2

DEDICATED TO THE SPIRITS AND THOSE
WHO CONSORT WITH THEM

Contents

Foreword   xiii

Introduction   1

Chapter 1   What Is a Spirit?   7

Chapter 2   Modes of Manifestation   23

Chapter 3   Spirit Skills   41

Chapter 4   Respect and Authority   55

Chapter 5   Prayers and Spells   71

Chapter 6   Get to Know the Locals   87

Chapter 7   Fear and Danger   105

Chapter 8   Friendly Conjuring   115

Chapter 9   Compelling Conjurations   145

Chapter 10   Intermediary Spirits and Familiars   171

Chapter 11   Relationships and Pacts   183

Chapter 12   Questions and Answers   197

Parting Words   213

Notes   215

Acknowledgments

First and foremost, I wish to thank my wife and children for their patience and encouragement during the writing of this book. When you throw writing a book on top of the demands of work, marriage, and parenting, it makes it harder on everyone. Their patience and support mean the world to me.

A very special thanks to my best friend and first student, artist and Sorcerer Matthew Brownlee, who provided the art for this book. My work would not be where it is without him.

Thanks to all my initiators, mentors, teachers, friends, and informants who opened their doors to me. Special thanks for this go to John Myrdhin Reynolds, Lopon Tenzin Namdak, Kunzang Dorje Rinpoche, Cliff and Misha Pollick, catherine yronwood, Tau Nemesius, Walter from the Globe, Paul Huson, and Blanch Krubner. You all opened yourselves up as mentors for me as a young man, and I would not be anywhere close to where I am today without your guidance.

Perhaps more than anyone I need to thank the students of Strategic Sorcery and all of the other programs that I run. Your questions, stories, and field reports give me the insight of a thousand Magicians instead of just my own. I would not be able to lead the life I do without you, so thank you.

Friends and peers who have been constant support and who let me bounce ideas off them are too numerous to mention, but I need to shout out to Mat Auryn, Christopher Bradford, Fabeku Fatunmise, Brianna Saussy, Aidan Watcher, BJ Swayne, James Foster, Sara Mastros, Jesse Hathaway, Jack Grayle, Jake Stratton Kent, and so many others who put up with me online and in person.

All of my books are guided by spirits; this one was guided most strongly by Astaroth, the first spirit I ever conjured, and who has held up her end of our pact for more than thirty years. The Goddess Hekate, who revealed a profound and detailed training that has now reached more than a thousand students. St Cyprian, Martyr and Magus, Sorcerer and Saint, who helped me to reconcile the forces of Christianity and Diabolism that have each pulled at me since I was a child.

I want to thank all at Weiser who worked on this book and who were extremely generous with deadline extensions.

Foreword

Standing at the crossroads, you can see the point of intersection between the right-hand path and left-hand path, the past and the future, religion, and blasphemy. It is the liminal point where opposites paradoxically meet—a middle ground from which to operate and choose the path you will travel down. Being the point where two roads intersect both literally and metaphorically, the crossroads has long been a symbol associated with the spirits of magick. Traditionally, one goes down to the crossroads to meet with a powerful spirit of magick. One might go there to make a deal with the devil or to work with the Goddess of witchcraft, Hekate, or to meet with the Iwa Papa Legba.

When I think of the crossroads, it's hard for me not to think of Jason Miller and his work. Not solely because of the spirits he works with that are associated with the crossroads but more so due to his approach to magic and more specifically, spirits in general. Several years back, I interviewed Jason Miller about his works and courses. I asked him why he embraced the word "Sorcerer" for himself over some of the more popular terms. He explained to me that for him, the term "Sorcerer" felt like a middle ground between the words "magician" and "witch." I would say Jason definitely stands where those two paths meet, potently working from the nexus of what appears to be often contradictory paths of magic and spiritism. From the crossroads' vantage point, he can see where these paths meet while also discerning where they diverge as separate and unique paths. In our interview, he explained that his approach was equally ceremonial and practical and that he valued intellect and intuition, knowledge, and experiential gnosis. You can see this even in how he approaches historically rooted ancient magick and enhances it with an innovative modern occult understanding and his own ingenious developments.

Like a modern-day Saint Cyprian of Antioch, Jason works with angels and demons, saints and heretics, Jesus and Lucifer, pagan and Buddhist Deities. You will find that same approach within this book. Yet, Jason allows for flexibility for you to work with the spirits that you are comfortable with engaging. I was first introduced to Jason Miller's books by another teacher of the Craft who had recommended them to me. The first book I read was *Protection and Reversal Magick*, and I quickly fell in love with it. Not only was this book the best I had read on the subject, but it was very focused on the ancient Titaness of magick and crossroads, Hekate. Synchronistically, this was at an auspicious time, as the spirit of Hekate had slowly started becoming a more substantial presence in my life. As such, I could easily integrate the material from the book into my personal practice with the relationship I was already developing with Hekate. Looking back, it's hard to not believe She was leading me to Jason's work.

A couple of years went by, and I decided to take one of the many courses he offers: the Sorcery of Hekate. This course remains one of the strongest influences on my approach to spirit work, with not just Hekate Herself, but with a whole horde of spirits. The Sorcery of Hekate has provided me with extremely effective tools that incorporate into my spiritual work to this day, as the results are palpable; and Jason's approach to magick has always been about results. Some of those approaches and techniques are in this very book, while there are so many more within these pages that aren't in his courses. This shouldn't be surprising at all due to Jason's extensive spiritual and magickal background and his earnest devotion and dedication to the spirits that he works with. It's only natural that he would have a clear understanding of what works and doesn't work when it comes to interacting with spirits through decades of trial and error.

But why should we learn how to work with spirits? Because, when you're a magickal practitioner, they're next to impossible to avoid. Right beneath the scope of ordinary perception exists a complex spiritual ecosystem composed of entities hidden to the naked eye. This ecosystem is interwoven with our physical ecosystem in terms of influence and interconnectedness. The complexity of the spirits that compose it ranges from simplistic entities with a mentality similar to that of our animal and plant kingdoms, or even machines, to more advanced entities adhering to complex hierarchical models with consciousnesses that exceed our own capabilities and understanding. Their influence undeniably affects us on the personal level and our larger culture, whether we're magickal practitioners or not. You wouldn't have to look far to find the influence of spirits on our religious systems, our cultural stories, and mythologies, or our entertainment.

The concept of incorporeal entities is so prevalent in our society that our language is painted with its usage, with an implicated assumption of the existence of spirits. We say that someone is in "high spirits" or "low spirits" when discussing their mood. If someone has stopped all communication, we say that they've ghosted us. If something is pleasurable, we refer to it as "divine," or if something is sinister, we refer to it as "diabolical." You can't even escape the spirits in a calendar, as most of our months are directly named after Gods and Goddesses or rituals focused on them. Even every single day of the week has the namesake of a deity. The examples are infinite. But spirits can have a much more direct influence upon us, for good or ill.

So how can we get a spirit to influence our lives in beneficial ways? How can we influence them? How do you call a spirit, and more importantly how can you ensure that the spirit hears you? Many books, including my own, will teach you how to see spirits. Where are books discussing how to be seen by the spirits? Where can we learn to discern spirits and gain rapport with the ones we want to work with and avoid the ones we don't want to work with? How can we recognize whether we have a genuine spiritual contact or a pure fabrication of our imaginations? How do we gain spiritual authority under a powerful spirit to compel or even exorcise problematic spirits? In this much-needed book, Jason Miller brilliantly answers and explores all of these topics and so much more. This is a book I wish I had fifteen years ago when I began working closely with spirits.

Working with spirits can be some of the most dangerous yet some of the most gratifying work a magickal practitioner can engage in. Jason understands this, and with Jason as your guide in this book, you are in some of the best hands out there when it comes to approaching and working with spirits.

Mat Auryn
author of *Psychic Witch: A Metaphysical Guide to Meditation, Magick, and Manifestation*
Antioch, CA—2021

Introduction

A few hundred years ago, doing anything this book recommends would have made you a criminal. The title of the book, *Consorting with Spirits*, is taken from the name of the crime you would have been charged with back in 17th-century England. More than a few men and women were tried, found guilty, and hanged for it.

Witch hysteria being what it is, most of the people they charged probably didn't do any actual conjuring or consorting with spirits, but many others did. We know from written testimony, as well as from surviving grimoires and manuals of Cunning people that, despite it being a crime, folks were trafficking with spirits. Let's take a moment to really appreciate this. Spirits were considered so important and powerful that people *risked imprisonment and execution* to contact them and communicate with them. The knowledge of how to manage this bridge between worlds was contraband of the highest order. The very knowledge you now hold in your hands.

So let's get down to some criminal undertakings, shall we?

Apart from a nod to the criminal charge faced by our predecessors, the other reason this book is called *Consorting with Spirits* is that it speaks to what I and most serious Magicians and Witches do throughout our lives. We don't just conjure a spirit once and ask for wisdom or boons, we *consort*. Merriam-Webster defines the verb "consort" as: *to keep company*. Cambridge Dictionary lists it as: *to spend a lot of time in the company of a particular group of people, especially people whose character is not approved of*. Oxford gives us the following definition: *habitually associate with (someone), typically with the disapproval of others*.

The key here is not the bit about bad character or disapproving authorities, though you will encounter both if you do this long enough, but the idea of keeping *habitual company*. Every successful Witch, Sorcerer, and Magician I know counts spirits among their list of friends, coworkers, and cohorts in the art. There is a relationship that develops between Sorcerer and spirit, and just like relationships with people, it can take many forms, each requiring its own type of care and cultivation.

You see, it's the *relationship* that really matters, not whether the spirit is in the correct column for the planet or whether the description in the book fits your needs. Those things matter for choosing spirits to make initial contact with, but that's just the starting point. Similar to relationships between people, something grows between you and a spirit you interact with regularly. You may find that a spirit associated with Venus, whom you initially contacted for help with love, winds up being much better for attracting customers to your business than a Jupiterian wealth spirit, if only because you have an established relationship already. You want to draw customers who will *love* what you offer, right?

This is also how some words of power and names that we cast spells and summon spirits with work. When you demand that a spirit appear in the name of Hekate Chthonos, Adonai, or Lucifer (or whichever power you are relying on), it's not simply name-dropping. Spirits can detect not only the investment you have in the power behind that name, but the investment that power has in *you*. That's relationship.

It is just as important to have relationships with the spirits where you live and work as it is to have relationships with well-known spirits who have their names and seals recorded in books. These are the spirits that you bump up against every day whether you, or they, know it or not. Reaching out to these spirits, introducing yourself, recording their names and information, and working together for the benefit of you both are among the most rewarding experiences available through magic. It's powerful too. When all is said and done, the best Sorcery is local.

As you go through this book, I will instruct you on how to conjure and communicate with spirits, but a lot of other books do that too. What I really hope to provide, and which I don't see enough of elsewhere, are the tools you need for *deepening* and *discerning* the communications that you receive.

Not all spirits tell the truth, and not everything that comes across during a communication is even a spirit at all. With the lessons from this book you will be able to separate reality from fantasy, truth from lies, and importance from insignificance. Once you know how to manage spirit communications, you can start to cut past surface-level visions and messages and get clear and actionable intelligence. It may be interesting that the Angel Tzadkiel brought an empowering vision of you sitting on a throne, but it's probably not very helpful in any practical way. Just like with people, cutting through the crap gets you to the good stuff that makes all this consorting with spirits worthwhile.

Anyone can perform a ritual or travel to a power spot and experience *something*. What I want is for you to experience *something that matters*.

A NOTE ON THE MAGIC IN THIS BOOK

People keep trying to put me and the magic I do in a box. "What tradition do you come from?" "What kind of magic do you do?" For good, or for ill, I am not that easy to nail down. I have been initiated in several traditions, but I am writing you here as a Sorcerer. In the end, the only thing that matters is if you can do the thing or not do the thing. Still, I should probably comment on the magic that I am bringing to you.

I am not one for wild eclecticism. I see a lot of misappropriation, strange connections, and cultural disrespect out there. If you are trying to call upon Jesus using the Phurba of Odin, you have strayed too far from any reasonable expression of truth or respect for the path. On the other hand, there are people who want to divide the world into neat boxes that never overlap or inform one another—keeping all things separate. The world is not neat and tidy and never has been.

I practice the magic that I have encountered naturally in my life. Even though I lived in a rural town in New Jersey, I somehow came into contact with a Rosicrucian teacher, a Rootwork mentor, a Witch, and a Tibetan Lama all before the age of twenty-one. For me to ignore the teachings I received from any of these people would be disrespectful, so I don't. To me, magic is magic. I no more worry about combining methods from these traditions that I have dedicated years of study to than I would about drawing lessons from French cooking and Tex-Mex at the same time. Food is food, and magic is magic.

In this book, I frame most of the rituals according to three points of view simultaneously:

Christianity. Most of the history of folk magic and grimoire magic in the West is written from this perspective.

Paganism. In this book, I focus on Hekate because I have a deep relationship with Hekate and many of my readers can adapt what I write into other Pagan perspectives.

Luciferianism. I consider this more or less connected to an esoteric view of Christianity. This is a stream that has informed a lot of my work with St Cyprian and one that is a growing sector of the magical community.

This may seem strange to people who want to hear from one perspective and one perspective only. I have been practicing magic for thirty years now, and these are just some of the rooms I have found myself in. We live in an age of global mass communication, and I won't pretend that we don't. The writers of the *Greek Magical Papyri* in 2nd-century Graeco-Roman Egypt Mediterranean managed to fuse Christian, Egyptian, Greek, Jewish, and Mithraic ideas in their practice. Can you *imagine* what they would have done if they'd had access to the internet?

These three approaches—the Christian, the Pagan, and the Luciferian—represent major streams of thought in the occult world that would benefit from a book like this. Other streams exist, and would certainly gain something from what is written here as well, but I am not planning on commenting on African traditional religions, Buddhism, or other approaches. Much of the magic in this book could be adapted to those lines of practice if one were clever.

Another reason to approach this topic from multiple angles is to show two important concepts: First, principles can be applied widely across almost any tradition of magic, or even magic worked entirely free of tradition. Second, some methods radically change depending upon the Gods and traditions invoked. In other words, principles are largely consistent throughout magic, but methods and tactics may need to change drastically depending on the forces involved and invoked.

THIS SHOULD NOT BE YOUR FIRST BOOK ON MAGIC

The last thing I want to mention is that this should probably not be your first book on magic. It's not that this is an advanced book; I plan on making things as simple and as straightforward as possible. It's simply that knowing some methods of protection, some basics of spellcraft, and having some competency at divination will make the work presented go a lot smoother. I already wrote a book about protection and reversal magic, so I don't plan on presenting a ton of shielding and protection methods here. That book, or just a few basic skills picked up in other places, will more than suffice for whatever this book might bring you into contact with.

Enjoy the book!

CHAPTER 1

What Is a Spirit?

In 1997 I completed a magical working aimed at making contact with my Holy Guardian Angel. This took nine months of increasingly longer and longer conjurations and prayers. The concept of making contact with a personal Angel that is unique to you comes from *The Book of the Sacred Magic of Abramelin the Mage,* but like most people, I was not following that text to the letter. My journey started using Aleister Crowley's Liber Samekh, and then reverting to the older ritual that Crowley based it on: The Rite of the Headless One. After months and months of dedicating the bulk of every day to attaining the Knowledge and Conversation of this spirit, I finally had done it. I could see and hear this Angel right there in the air in front of me. It was *glorious.*

After giving me her name, she asked what tool I would conjure the Demons with.

"Uhhhh. I don't believe in the concept of Angels and Demons as a dichotomy," I said. "So I was not planning on doing that."

The Angel's reply was a little shocking: "It doesn't really matter what you believe, Jason. You need to do it tomorrow or your life is gonna go to shit. I will find you a tool."

I was not used to spirits telling me my beliefs don't really matter. At that point in time, I was pretty convinced that applied belief was what magic was all about, so this came as a shock. This was new. This "Holy Guardian Angel" that I thought might just be a deep part of my own mind—perhaps a mystical state of being connected to the divine—clearly was a lot more independent than I originally thought. The Angel said it would give me a tool. I wondered what that meant.

That evening my roommate and I had some Magician friends over. One of them decided to give a gift more or less out of the blue: a five-foot-tall Egyptian-style Was-Scepter that he had been working on for months. I could not believe that he was giving me this incredible thing he had spent so much time on. Then I remembered the Angel's promise: a magical tool to bind Demons within twenty-four hours! Clearly there was more to this spirit than I thought. There is nothing quite like getting taken to school by something you don't particularly believe in.

WHAT ARE SPIRITS?

I mentioned in the introduction that "consorting with spirits" was once the name of a crime. The assumption at that time was that spirits were fully formed and independent beings who existed in their own realms somewhat adjacent to ours. Like you and me, but different. Some spirits were thought to wander our world like restless ghosts or Demons looking to cause harm. Others might be contacted only through access points like caves or Fairy circles. You always had people who did not believe in the existence of spirits at all, but for those who did believe, and those who felt their influence, spirits were as real as you or I. *But what precisely are they?*

Before I give my own answer to this question, let me give a crash course in the ever-changing models of spirits and magic throughout the last few centuries.

MAGIC'S NEXT TOP SPIRIT MODEL

The scientific Enlightenment rocked the world, dispelling all sorts of notions that we once held as common fact. Decade after decade, our idea of how the world worked was torn down and rebuilt by science. It was not long after Galileo was tried for supporting the idea that Earth revolved around the sun that it became commonly accepted fact. The idea that maggots did not just magically arise from rotting meat was proven, and spontaneous generation was thrown into the trash bin of bad ideas. Germs were found to be a more reliable cause of disease than Demons, and something as simple as washing hands became one of the greatest lifesaving advancements in human history.

In this new world that sent Aristotle spinning in his grave and the Church scrambling for relevancy, the existence of spirits no longer seemed a given in the mind of the public. Ironically, the same period that saw these giant leaps in scientific knowledge is also the period that most of the classical grimoires were written: *The Picatrix, The Grimoire Verum, The Ars Goetia,* and *The Keys of Solomon*. Those who worked magic continued to see and consort with spirits, but because science was allowing people to think about the world differently, perhaps it was time for Magicians to think a bit differently about spirits.

THE EMERGENCE OF THE MIND MODEL

Witches and Magicians find themselves in a quandary: How do we engage Witchcraft, Magic, and Sorcery while also embracing the scientific wonders of the world? Magic is not merely religion; after all, we cannot simply rely on faith. Anyone that does magic a few times knows that magic works, even if they cannot fully explain *how* it works. Spirits, being a large part of magic, would undergo a radical review by the Witches and Magicians of the 1800s and 1900s.

The emerging discipline of psychology provided models of the mind that seemed endlessly deep. Perhaps spirits have been projections of the mind all along—a way that Sorcerers interact with the world. If dreams are the mind creating characters and images that reveal information to itself, perhaps spirits are like waking dreams? Aleister Crowley suggested this more than once. In his introduction to his edition of the *Goetia of Solomon* he wrote:

> The spirits of the Goetia are portions of the human brain. Their seals therefore represent (Mr. Spencer's projected cube) methods of stimulating or regulating those particular spots (through the eye). The names of God are vibrations calculated to establish: (a) General control of the brain.

When Carl Jung proposed "collective unconscious" (a deep part of the unconscious mind inherited from our ancestors rather than subjectively shaped by ourselves), Magicians saw not only that spirits could be explained by a psychological model of magic, but that this might even explain the ways that spirits seemed to behave beyond our own minds. It was an exciting idea that interfaced with science a lot better than invisible friends hiding in Fairy mounds or a world populated with Demons that have nothing better to do than tempt people.

The Energy Model

While our inner worlds were being explored by psychologists, our outer world was being re-shaped by harnessing different types of invisible forces. Electricity started to illuminate our world and radio waves were being used to communicate to masses of people over long distances. This age of energy also provided an interesting model for how magic could work. If you could turn on a radio or light switch and have invisible forces create light and sound, perhaps instead of spirits it was an invisible force that was at work in magical operations. In Indian and Tibetan magic, which the

West was starting to take renewed interest in, the idea of manipulating energy has been integral for hundreds of years. This was an attractive explanation of magic that resonated with the modern world of the 20th century.

These models of the late 19th and early 20th century helped usher in some vast changes to how people practiced magic. Whereas magic used to be worked alone or in very small groups, suddenly large movements were organizing around magical ideas. The group-based masonic-style lodge system started to pop up all over Europe and then spread to the Americas. This is also the time that saw Margaret Murray's thesis on the survival of a Witch cult give rise to many Covens, and eventually the now widespread religions of Wicca and other strands of Neo-Paganism. Instead of a secret solo endeavor, occultism was becoming respectable. Well . . . almost.

Because of the popularity and acceptability of the mind and energy models, spirits began to play a reduced role in these movements compared to older magics. Indeed, spells and sorcery seemed to become almost beside the point. One could be a Magician and focus entirely on spiritual growth. One could practice Witchcraft religiously and never cast a spell. Practical magic meant to produce a measurable result started to get sidelined. Of course, there were still plenty of practical Sorcerers out there. Mastering Witchcraft, as well as hoards of spellbooks, were still published for those who wanted to actually better their lives with magic. Rootwork and folk magic never went anywhere either, and held a more traditional view of spirits. This is how things went through most of the 20th century.

CHAOS AND RESULTS

By the 1980s a movement emerged that sought to return results-oriented magic to the spotlight. Chaos Magic seemed to be defined more by what it rejected than by what it embraced. It rejected the masonic claptrap of magical orders, as well as the focus on religious faith of the growing Neo-Pagan movement. To the Chaos Magician it did not matter *what* you believed in; it was *belief itself* that did the heavy lifting of magic. According to this model, Scrooge McDuck would work as well as Jupiter for a wealth magic working, as long as you could focus enough *belief* and will through that lens.

The 1990s saw the world of magic divided between the old spirit model, a psychological model, an energy model, and other new models such as an information model or cyber model, which reflected the influence of the internet. Chaos Magicians posed a new option that would resolve the disputes between these seemingly exclusionary models: the meta model.

Chaos Magicians of the '90s loved anything "meta." Rather than viewing magic as working through spirits or mind or energy, Chaos Magic suggested that because belief was the primary factor in magic, one could switch between these by investing belief in whatever suited your work. The meta model of magic was like a quantum state that would only take shape once it was observed by the Magician. Nineties-era Chaos Magicians love anything "quantum" almost as much as we loved anything "meta."

If all that sounds confusing as hell, well, it kind of is. Even though Chaos Theory and quantum physics had been around for eighty years, this futuristic-sounding and post-modern view appealed to the Magicians facing the milestone of the looming millennium. The future, we were told, was very nearly at hand.

BEYOND Y2K

Thankfully as we all settled into the new millennium, Magicians, Witches, and other magical folk began to see through this complicated and convoluted quantum entanglement of occult theories. If there was a trend that marked the magic of the new millennium, it was a *return to tradition*. The last twenty years have seen dozens of English translations of old grimoires and magical workbooks. Classics like the sixth and seventh books of Moses and *The Book of the Sacred Magic of Abramelin the Mage* got re-issued with new scholarship, correcting many errors and misunderstandings. Witches began to investigate traditional craft outside of the Wiccan/Neo-Pagan bubble.

Western magic, which has largely been a tradition in text more than person-to-person lineage, began to open its eyes to the rest of the world and its living traditions. Interest in taking initiations in living magical traditions rooted in Asia, Africa, and the Caribbean continues to grow. Most importantly, spirits are once again viewed by most magical practitioners as real and independent beings rather than mental projections or energetic patterns. I view this as a very good thing. Even most modern Chaos Magicians have incorporated the reality of spirits into their paradigm. Sadly, like most good things, people take it too far. Advocates of the revived spirit model now assert their supremacy over those who incorporate any view of mind or energy into their magic. To them, all magic of any kind is performed by spirits.

A MEGA MODEL

In my view, we never needed a "meta model," because none of these models were ever exclusive in the first place. I mentioned that energy and mind both play a huge role in Asian magical systems, but so do spirits. There is no need for a model that reduces magic to *one* function. Arguing about whether magic works exclusively through the intercession of spirits versus mind or energy is like debating whether your car works exclusively via gasoline versus electricity or oil. The car requires *all* these elements as facets of its operation. So, too, is it with magic. The view needs to be *mega*, not meta. We need a large view where spirits are real and active, but the role of mind and energy is also important. These are important, not only because it explains how magic works, but also because *you are a spirit too.* . . .

SO, WHAT IS A SPIRIT?

I promised to answer this question at the start of this chapter, didn't I? If we are going to accept that spirits are real, as has been the view of Magicians pretty much everywhere throughout all time except in the 19th- to 20th–century English-speaking West, then we need to nail down what we are talking about. Let's not kid ourselves; we can accept that spirits are real, and even that they are independent, but we must also acknowledge that they exist in a way that is more subtle and fluid than a human or a horse. Fluid or not, we need some kind of operating definition if we are going to work with them. Here is what I suggest: spirits are organized consciousness.

It's that simple. Merriam-Webster defines consciousness as a state or quality of being characterized by sensation, emotion, volition, and thought.[1] I am more or less an animist. I think the universe is conscious. All space and time, pregnant with formless awareness that can organize in endless ways. I don't know all the ways and I don't pretend to. Frankly, I think that there are more ways than we even *can* know. But let's brainstorm a few vectors of organization anyway.

The consciousness of humans and animals is organized most obviously according to a physical body. Humans are spirits too, after all. If we take this simple idea and run with it outside of a purely materialist view, our own consciousness can be organized along a number of different models apart from just the brain. For instance, if we acknowledge reincarnation, we have to allow for consciousness to reorganize itself in new brains and experiences, yet still have some connection to what came before. A subtle structure that we might term a "soul." If we accept Astral Projection, we have to allow for consciousness to be organized, at least for a while, outside the body.

Do plants have consciousness? Some botanists think they do,[2] and others are not so sure. What about rocks? What about space? Different spiritual traditions hold different opinions, but it is this essentially animist view that Magicians and Witches are returning to in 2022—that all the world is alive with spirit.

Let's take a look at different factors that impact the organization of consciousness and how this affects the way that spirits manifest.

TRADITION

If we call upon the Archangel Michael, we are looking at a spirit that is truly vast in reach, as witnessed by people all over the world who attest to his powerful intercession. How is it organized? Are Archangels self-organized or does the tradition a spirit comes from take a part in the organization of the spirit?

I believe there is a reality behind the spirit that is beyond what we humans have said about him, but at the same time I think the name and the images and stories we know can't be fully separated from us.

In Buddhist Magic, you have a mix of spirits that have all been organized, at least partially, by varied traditions. You have Siddhas and Gurus who were once living humans. You have local non-Buddhist spirits who have been "converted" (some willingly, some by force) into guardians of the tradition, who still also answer to their non-converted protocols in those religions. Add to this a dizzying variety of enlightened spirits, whose different forms and mantras are meant to aid in different ways: Kurukulla to subjugate, Dzambhala to increase wealth, Phurba to nail down obstacles, and so on. These beings are defined and organized almost entirely by the tradition that they arise and develop within. Is there something to these spirits that pre-dates human worship and contact or are they organized entirely by us? I suspect there is, but can't say for sure. There is more to them than what any individual thinks of them. Just because a spirit may have been born or organized around human need does not mean that they exist only in *your* head.

Some people feel that spirits are organized and defined by the human traditions and cultures they arise within. But just because one or more traditions are part of a spirit's identity doesn't mean

What Is a Spirit?

that there is no real and independent being at the heart of it. Think about your own life. When you are at work, isn't your consciousness organized a little differently than when you are on a date? How about a fight? Even the time of day can affect the "you" I would get if I called you on the phone. If these things can affect the nature of a consciousness rooted in a physical body, then how much deeper might that principle hold for a more subtle being like a spirit that is not contained by a physical body?

ORGANIZED BY LOCATION

The spirit of the stream that runs through my property here in Vermont is a lot more localized than an Archangel. Unlike Michael or Raphael, she's unconcerned with tradition or religion. Her locality is the key to her presence. If I were to share her name and call her from wherever you are, I don't think that we would get her. We might get something, but I doubt it would be the spirit of this stream.

When I lived in the Pine Barrens of New Jersey, I worked heavily with the ghost of a local Witch named Peggy Clevenger who passed in the 1800s. She showed me how to call upon the spirit known as the Jersey Devil, a famous cryptid that is a like a guardian spirit of the area. Some believe the Jersey Devil is the result of a woman named Mother Leeds cursing or promising her thirteenth child to the Devil. Others believe the spirit to be much older. A being that caused the Lenape to call the Pine Barrens "Popuessing," the place of the dragon. Acting on a local legend that the Jersey Devil would manifest where stunted pines overlook pools of deep blue, I hiked out to one of the blue holes— mysterious pools of titanium blue water that stay unnaturally cold even in summer. With this location and instructions from Peggy, I successfully conjured the spirit. I could never invoke the Jersey Devil anywhere except that location. I tried from my home, but to no avail. Now that I live several states away from New Jersey, I can no longer call upon Peggy Clevenger either. Both spirits are organized very highly by their location; they exist very close to the physical and are bound by it.

We aren't ready to talk practical magic yet, so ask yourself the following question first. What is better for magic: a spirit that is hyper-local who may not be well known or incredibly powerful, or a vast and powerful spirit who is busy with people all over the world? I am not going to answer that one for you. It's just food for thought. But if you think in terms of whether it's better to have a famous and powerful person versus a local person on your side, the answer is usually that it depends on the problem. Thinking about questions like this is more important than arriving at a definitive answer.

At times, spirits who are clearly organized around a specific location grow to become accessible by people all over the world. Even so, they may get more immanent at the location they are connected with. The Shvanamukha Sisters appeared to the great Sorcerer Padmasambhava in what is now Pharping, Nepal. Despite being connected to that location, they get invoked as protectors daily by every practitioner of Vajrakilaya the world over and are integral to the magic of the Phurba, the three-sided dagger. I have invoked them, felt their presence, and successfully called upon them for magic from here in the United States for years. But when I lived for a month in Pharping, and regularly visited the Asura Cave where they were bound by Padmasambhava, I actually saw them and spoke to them in a way that is far more visceral than how they manifest here.

This is not unique to Buddhism, of course. Many spirits are called upon all over the world, yet manifest most strongly at special shrines and locations that act as portals. Mary at Medjugorje, Bosnia and Herzegovina, and Lourdes, France, for instance. This is one reason that pilgrimage is such a potent magical act. Sometimes you can carry the influence of a place with you like a souvenir. Rosaries from Medjugorje or dirt from the Asura Cave help tune in to these presences.

ORGANIZED BY BEHAVIOR

Certain spirits are organized by behaviors. Spirits of wrath, spirits of peace, spirits of lust, spirits of purity, and so on. In a lot of traditional medicine and prayer, different behaviors are thought to be spurred by spirits who encourage those behaviors. Extreme examples would be written up as cases of possession or obsession. I don't know that I am ready to blame people's behaviors on spirits quite yet, but I do know that like attracts like.

If you are the type of person who likes to party with rough and dangerous people, you are going to seek them out and they seek you out, and you all double down on the behavior that bonds you. A houngan from Haiti once explained that the Petro nation of lwa arose from the need for spirits wrathful enough to pull off a slave revolt. Spirits from the Congo and other nations were given very specific offerings and rituals that would attract spirits who had that nature and help bring it out in others. It was the most successful and lasting slave revolt in history.

Matthew Brownlee, the illustrator for this book, is working now on an oracle deck of spirits, some of which are arranged or representative of behaviors. The image on the next page is his depiction of a spirit and seal that embodies addiction.

INDEPENDENTLY ORGANIZED

There are also beings that are not material, at least in a way that we understand material, yet are not organized by anything other than themselves or perhaps parented much in the same way that we are. Every indigenous culture that I know of has a catalogue of different categories of spirits. These are not like books of individual spirits, but rather classifications of spirit races and how they behave, appear, are offended, are pleased, and so on. In Scotland, you have the Seelie and Unseelie Court, which more or less means the happy or unhappy and bad Fairies. In Wales, you have Ellyllon (elves), Bwbachod (household spirits), Colbynau (of the underground), Gwyllion (of the mountains), and so on. In Greece,

you have all manner of Nymphs that populate pools, mountains, and gardens. In India and Tibet, you have Yakshas of the earth, Nagas of freshwater, Gandharvas of air, and a nearly endless host of other spirits one might encounter. The situation is similar to Japan, with their Yokai and Kama.

In some cases, these spirits may be tied to a specific place, but more often than not it is simply just the place where they have made their home. A spirit *in* the lake, not *of* the lake, if you catch my meaning.

These spirits can be useful as allies, and can also become enemies if mistreated. A good amount of traditional medicine is devoted to pacifying or exorcising the influence of spirits who are just as independent as us, and whose lives overlap with ours in ways that we may not fully understand.

EMBRACE COMPLEXITY

You can probably think of other ways that consciousness may be organized. Most spirits, especially famous and powerful ones, are organized along the lines I listed and more. Spirits of planetary influence, spirits of specific times, and so on.

Some spirits behave quite differently under different circumstances. The Sorcery of Hekate course I teach works with Hekate in a very specific, secret, and unique way, but does not represent the entirety of what Hekate is. She clearly manifests differently to different people at different times. The Hekate who can curse your neighbor's horse written about in the Defixiones Tablets can seem hard to reconcile with the very transcendent Hekate of the Chaldean Oracles, yet she is the same being. She behaves differently when called upon in different ways. The same is true of St Cyprian, who gets called upon by Orthodox Christians, Sorcerers, and Quimbandeiros alike. Each one is a "different Cyprian" yet still the same being.

Satan or Lucifer may mean something entirely evil to a devout Christian, but represent freedom and liberation to people who have been marginalized or victimized by the Church. Is he a fallen Angel? A dark Lord of Witchcraft? A serpent who delivers knowledge? My answer is yes, all the above.

Does this all seem messy to you? Did you notice I did not fully and completely explain it all into a neat little package? Good! Magic is real, spirits are real, and anything real is rarely well served by being placed into a tidy box and wrapped with a bow. Embrace the fact that there is not only more about spirits than we know, but more than we *can* know. If we embrace a little humility with our practice, it gives a lot of room to grow and operate. It's the first step to really know what spirits are.

CHAPTER 2

Modes of Manifestation

Have you ever noticed that a great stand-up comedian can deliver jokes on stage that would ordinarily be offensive, yet have that audience laughing and not taking the slightest offense at otherwise racy material? This is because they have spent years learning to deliver jokes to an audience in person. Everyone leaves the club happy. The same routine done as a Netflix special may still work, but without the social proof that comes from being in front of a crowd, it may not. When that joke gets written down without the benefit of the comedian's skills or facial expressions, that same material will be offensive because what people see are just the words on the page.

What does this have to do with spirits? Simple: Every interaction you have with another person is colored by who you are, who they are, and the medium through which you are communicating. If communication can be this subtle for people, how much more so is it for subtle beings like spirits? This is why it's not enough to know what a spirit is. We need to also know the ways in which they manifest.

ORIENTATION

The world is filled with spirits, but you may have noticed that they don't make the news much. Traffic jams aren't caused by specters blocking up the intersection. People don't call the police because the ghost of the town peeping tom is looking in on them. If during a powerful conjuration the Angel Tzadkiel appears to the conjuror as a six-story-tall column of fire, the fire department is usually not called. This is because there are different layers to reality, and different beings are naturally oriented toward different layers.

In my book *The Sorcerer's Secrets*, I gave a three-level division: Physical, Astral, and Empyrian or Spiritual. This works for a lot of things, but in this book it's helpful to parse this out a bit more into seven levels or layers of reality.

Physical: This is the hard-edged world we all know. Three dimensions of space. We experience time moving forward. Movement requires physical exertion of some kind.

Etheric: A layer between the physical and astral. It can't be detected by physical implements but is not entirely separate either. If you think of winds and channels in yoga or meridians in acupuncture, these are nonphysical structures that require physical exertion to effect. Breath and muscle are used in things like yoga and qi-gung. Needles or pressure are used in acupuncture and moxibustion.

Astral: Still experiencing three dimensions of space, but things are a lot more malleable. You can effect the astral through application of the will and imagination. This is why those who warn of the dangers of the astral consider it like a maze of mirrors; it can easily reflect our hopes and fears. There are multiple levels covered here, ranging from a layer that closely mirrors the physical,[1] to lands so alien that they have almost no relation to our world. It is my belief that many different etheric and physical universes connect at this level. This is, for lack of a better term, "the other side."

Symbol Space: Just as the etheric level bridges the physical and the astral, this level bridges the astral and mental levels. It is at this level that pure information manifests into space and the higher subtler levels of astral space collapse into pure manifestation. It is from this level that the more effective seals, sigils, mandalas, and magical circles come. Pure information expressed symbolically and spacially.

Mental: It is here that we should stop using the term "space" because there really is no spatial distance. Things simply are. In the 1800s theosophists described this level as "The Akashic records" and conceptualized it as a library. I think a better analogy is available now: programming code. Symbol space and the astral can be thought of as websites with a graphical user interface, but underneath that is just lines of code. It's a rough analogy, but useful. In the end you need to experience this yourself.

Causal: At this state even the concept of subject-object starts to break down. It is a bridge between the mental level and what lies underneath everything. It is here that existence as we know it starts to, well, exist.

Perfection: I don't want to say much about this. Is it God? Is it Void? Is it Emptiness? Is it Fullness? By definition, it is beyond duality and is the providence of mystics and perhaps one day physicists. I will let you draw your own conclusions.

Why are these levels important? Because every being in existence is oriented to one of these levels naturally. Despite being naturally oriented to that level, they exist at all the levels above it. So a spirit that is naturally manifest in the astral also manifests at the symbol space, mental, causal, and perfection levels. Humans and animals naturally oriented to the physical level also exist on all the levels above it.

The trick to consorting with spirits is doing the work necessary to form a bridge between their natural orientation point and ours. This may be a simple communication from one level to another. It may be that a spirit manifests to your physical senses. It can be you stretching your senses to meet a spirit at their orientation point. Often it is a meeting somewhere in the middle.

As we cover the different levels of manifestation in this chapter, and the different modes of communication throughout this book, keep this concept of orientation in mind. It will help you choose the methods that will best achieve your goals, and enable you to have greater understanding while consorting with spirits.

MANIFESTATION MATTERS

When people are in a haunted place, they can often point to where in the room they sense a ghost. It's over *there* . . . . By contrast, when people pray to Deities, guardians, or Angels, they often simply feel a presence within or around them rather than in a specific corner of the room. My experience of magical invocation is that powerful spirits tend to manifest first as a presence and then need to be directed into a particular place to manifest. Sometimes this is done by request and other times by force, but we can get into that later.

Some mystics feel a union or an overlap with a spirit or a God, as if they are simultaneously the same being yet still individual. Another experience some have is of traveling bodily, astrally, or in vision to the abode of a spirit and communicating with them on their own turf.

Each of these types of manifestations facilitates very different experiences and proves useful in different ways. As if this were not complicated enough, each of these manifestations can be triggered by the spirit or the Magician through a wide variety of means.

I believe that anything from reaching out with the mind to full-blown multi-hour rituals can produce authentic manifestations of spirits, but that doesn't mean that these things are equal. If anything has been missing from the discussion on spirits, it is embracing the complex array of possible interactions.

Imagine that a new neighbor moved in. Do you call them on the phone? Do you drop a note? Do you go over and introduce yourself? Do you wait for them to make the first move? Do you give a gift? Do you ignore them unless there is a conflict? Consider how the medium of contact would affect your relationship with this new neighbor. Now you have some idea of why different modes of manifestation matter.

I have created a classification system that I think serves the needs of a 21st-century spirit worker quite well. What's important to realize is that, as with most classification systems, it's a way of making sense of something that is very fluid and dynamic so that it can be useful. Systems like this are not complete or inherently true, so you may come across experiences that bridge these classifications, or defy them totally. As Alfred Korzybski noted,

> A map is not the territory it represents, but, if correct, it
> has a similar structure to the territory, which accounts for
> its usefulness.[2]

Now that you know this is just a map and not the terrain, let's take a quick tour of the maps of manifestation.

MANIFESTATIONS OF RESONANCE

The first spirit I ever called upon with the intent of getting something in return might have been Paralda, King of the Air Elementals. I was fifteen years old and using methods from Al Manning's *Helping Yourself with White Witchcraft*. Not a book I would choose or recommend now, but I wasn't old enough to drive and webpages hadn't been invented yet, so my options were limited.

When I did it, I felt a general change in the atmosphere, like the air had become charged somehow. I suppose I could dismiss that as a fantasy of a teenage brain that desperately wanted magic to be real because the spirit did nothing to make itself known otherwise. No wind crashing through the window. No voice whispering "It shall be done" in my ear. The crazy thing, however, is that what I asked for was done. The dispute that I invoked him to influence was settled in my favor. The magic I asked him to do worked.

So this begs the question: Was Paralda, King of Air Elementals, there in my bedroom among my cassette tapes and *Thrasher* magazines on the floor? I don't think so. I think I experienced what I call a manifestation of resonance.

What is resonance? In sound, it is the reflection from a surface by the synchronous vibration of a neighboring object. If I am in a room full of guitars and strum an E chord on one of them, the others will resonate with that chord. Something similar happens when you pray. It's not that a God suddenly stops what they are doing and appears before you in full mind-breaking, gray-hair-inducing fullness. You resonate with that power and the universe responds. If that resonance is made firm in actions like burning candles or herbs with the right properties, writing a petition, or nailing down something ritually, then your prayer is elevated into something else: a spell.

This level of manifestation, simple resonance, is the most commonplace manifestation of a spirit's influence in your life. It accounts for probably 80 percent of magic. Even in some classical grimoires that focus on making spirits appear, active resonance is all that is sought. A handbook confiscated during the Venetian Inquisition in 1636[3] is filled with spells that use the seals of Demons that appear in the *Grimoire Verum*, but don't require the spirit's appearance. To attract money, for instance, we are told to cut circles of parchment the size of the desired coins and place the seal of Claunth on them, place them into a circle, and recite a short incantation to Claunth:

> Claunth feras catelam
> Pignuth mentheranot agan
> Securma ferunt erithren
> Clebanot nechin Trebren

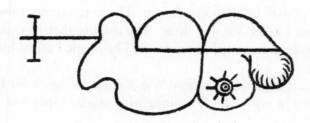

Claunth doesn't actually need to appear or agree to anything. He may or may not even be aware of his influence being used this way. Yet, it is being used. Like the woman who touched the hem of Christ's garment and withdrew some of his power to heal herself, we are grabbing the power of a Demon and tying it to this magical action, which will then hopefully manifest.

This is the most minor way that a spirit can manifest, but let me be clear: *this is often all that is needed*. Just because there are stronger ways for a spirit to manifest in your life, that doesn't make those methods preferable. I sometimes see people bragging about two- or three-hour ceremonies of evocation that pull a spirit into visible appearance in order to accomplish something that most people could easily manifest with a bit of folk magic, or just some non-magical elbow grease. The power of resonance should not be underrated.

But there is much more. . . .

INHABITATION

Every day thousands of people all over the world do a ritual called the Lesser Banishing Ritual of the Pentagram. It's probably the most famous and widespread practice to emerge from the Order of the Golden Dawn. During this ritual, you channel the power of the Divine through your own body, draw pentagrams in the air that are charged with names of God, then visualize four Archangels standing at the quarters of the circle and call their names to inhabit those forms.

Before me Raphael, Behind me Gabriel, On my Right Hand Michael, On my left hand Uriel, for about me flames the Pentagram, and Within me shines the six-rayed star.

What's happening when people do this? Are those Archangels coming in the fullness of their presence to stand around you? I don't think so, and everything ever written about the majesty of angelic presence would suggest otherwise as well. Yet something beyond mere resonance is happening. I call this *Inhabitation*.

You aren't just calling the names of the Angels for their influence, you are visualizing them in a particular way and then asking them to inhabit that visualization. The visualization you choose is not only a way of giving the power of the Archangel somewhere to go, but patterns the manifestation by the colors, and implements, and symbols—telling the form how to act and what you want them to do.

A more complex version of this is carried out in Vajrayana Buddhism where symbolic beings are generated by the practitioner, then through invocation are merged with actual beings. In Inner Tantras, the central visualized being is the practitioner, which changes it a bit from simple inhabitation (we will talk more about it later).

Of course, visualizations are not the only things that spirits can inhabit. They can inhabit statues, ikons, symbols, and items of the art. When I wrote "Sorcerer's Call to St Cyprian of Antioch" in 2013, I prayed it nine times every day for the nine days preceding his feast day on September 26.[4] Each night I could tell that St Cyprian was present because the statue would appear to come to life. I started calling this odd phenomena—a statue or ikon seeming to move even though it really isn't—the Harryhausen Effect, named after the famous master of monster animation Ray Harryhausen. When the statue would jump to life like this, I knew that I could communicate requests, and that if I reached out, I could get answers back from the good Sorcerer Saint as well.

A Sorcerer can take this idea of inhabitation to another level and create a permanent spirit house. Some spirits are invited to take up residence and receive offerings at these structures willingly, and others are coaxed and trapped in them. Either case is still inhabitation, though these permanent-style residences require a lot more finesse and experience than we are ready to present in this chapter. Suffice to say that they require a good bit of knowledge to make correctly, and a serious dedication to upkeep.

The main point to remember about inhabitation is that the spirit is this: a spirit is filling a vessel you provide and acting according to the parameters set by that vessel—be it a temporary visualization, a phsysical statue for veneration, or a complex spirit house.

CONTROLLED APPEARANCE

> I powerfully command you through the strong and
> wonderful names El, Elohim, Adonai, Tzabaoth, that you
> appear before this circle in a fair visible human form and
> without tortuosity . . .
>
> —*The Clavis Inferni*

This quote is from *The Clavis Inferni*, a grimoire attributed to St Cyprian. Similar instructions are contained in almost every classical conjuration: demanding that the spirit appear in a beautiful or affable form and that it refrain from causing trouble. The *Verus Jesuitarum Libellus* specifies that the spirit abstain "wholly from all harm, without noise, lightning, or tempest, without terror and trembling." This is what I call manifestation through controlled appearance.

Controlled appearance is when a spirit manifests in a form that is negotiated between the Sorcerer and the spirit, usually within the context of a conjuration or evocation where the spirit is expected to appear, either at the edge of a circle or in a scrying device like a crystal or mirror.

The key here is that while manifestations of spirits through resonance *may* be accompanied by omens and dreams, and spirit habitations *may* be accompanied by any number of communications from the spirit, controlled appearances are defined by the two-way communication between spirit and conjuror. The reason it is "controlled appearance" rather than just appearance is that the parameters for communication are set by the Sorcerer, Witch, or Magician who is calling the spirit. Rather than allowing the spirit to show up however it likes, care is taken to request that it takes on a form that is not frightening to the operator.

Don't get too hung up on the visuals though. Some of the bombastic descriptions of Demons in classical grimoires would certainly make for great cinema, but that is not the only way spirits can manifest. Sometimes a spirit will not appear as easily as they can speak, and you will have auditory rather than visual communication. Still, the spirit should be bound by the parameters of the conjuration or ritual that they were called by. As Chas Chandler said to John Constantine in the movie *Constantine*, "It's not always like it is in the books, is it?"

When I was sixteen years old, I contacted the Demon Astaroth using instructions in *The Complete Book of Magic and Witchcraft* by Kathryn Paulsen, which she pulled out of the *Grimoire Verum*, a book I did not have back in 1988. After laying out the circle and reading the conjurations seven times, I felt a hand on the back of my neck and a voice whisper to me from behind. It had a bit of a creep factor. I reminded him that he was not supposed to cross the circle. At that moment I felt the hand withdraw and the voice become a little more distant, as it informed me that "he" was a "she."

When I asked her to appear in a pleasing form, she did. It looked something like the drawing on the next page.

I have used numerous methods to communicate with Astaroth throughout the years, and thirty years later, she remains as much a part of my life as some human friends and acquaintances. This is the beauty of two-way communication. Real relationships form and magic takes on a deeper dimension than just requests to spirits.

MANIFESTATIONS OF TRUE SPIRITS

> Kid . . . have you got nine tongues? Tongues kid, have
> you got nine of them? Is your mouth more than six feet
> wide? No? Then give it up. It's an alien language, your
> little skin flap of a mouth can't handle it.
> —*Chthulhu, from Calls for Chthulhu, Episode One*

This was the answer that Chthulhu gave to a caller who wanted
to pronounce his name correctly on the hilarious web show, *Calls
for Chthulhu*. It's a joke, but it's also kind of true. I once asked the
Angel Camael (Khammael), who I had conjured using methods
from Trithemius's *The Art of Drawing Spirits into Crystals*, what his true
name was (a name not influenced by human tradition, but his *real*
name). He very cheekily asked me if I had twelve vocal cords, and
if not, I shouldn't worry about it.

See, that's the thing about spirits. We all want the real authentic unfiltered thing, but we aren't really built for it. When it comes
to beings oriented to those subtler levels, what they lack in physi-
cality, they make up for in subtleness, vastness, and (from our perspective) weirdness. That kind of mind-bending experience can
be traumatic, which is why Magicians often demand that the spirit
appear in a comely form. It's also why a consistent theme among
records of evocations is that spirits want the experience of being
conjured over with as soon as possible.

When you do get a true appearance, or at least an appearance
chosen without the input of the human, it is usually initiated by
the spirit rather than a Magician, or it is the result of mystical
practice. For our purposes here the main differentiator between
mysticism and magic lies in the role of effort versus effortlessness.
The Magician or Witch makes an effort with a ritual or conjuration and often repeats it many times, whereas a mystic opens
themselves up to a presence and lets go more and more.

This is not to say that the true appearance of all spirits is very
difficult to behold. Ezekiel's Angels may be interlocking wheels

of eyes, Avalokiteshvara might have eleven heads and a thousand arms, and the genius of the forest I live in looks like a swirling mass of green that phases in and out of reality, but that doesn't mean every spirit looks as strange as these spirits. The possibilities are endless, including the possibility that they look just like a person or an animal. The point of me listing true appearance as a way that spirits manifest is to show that there are scenarios in which *they* are in control of the scenario, *not you*. You may be averse to ever allowing such a scenario to arise, and indeed a lot of Magicians have been taught to always maintain the strictest control over everything. Suffice to say that I respectfully disagree. I don't manage the people in my life this way, and I don't manage all spirits this way either. To each their own, though.

POSSESSION

Everything I have covered so far has been about spirits manifesting separately from us—either as a presence, indwelling something, or appearing in front of you. But what about calling a spirit to come and dwell *in* you? Spirits, Demons, and Gods have been taking possession of mortals throughout history. Such indwelling of spirits can be unwanted and the cause for all manner of physical and mental ills. The Testament of Solomon, one of the earliest examples of Solomonic Spirit Catalogues that influenced later grimoires like the *Key of Solomon*, begins with spirits exorcised from an unfortunate victim. Then the spirits are questioned on their roles, powers, and ruling Angels, so in a way possession and exorcism are at the root of that tradition.

Of course, there are those who welcome possession. For these folks, it is a sublime act of devotion that benefits all parties. The entity gains a comfortable foothold into the physical, the possessed is changed spiritually and magically by the possession, and the community gains an audience with a spirit who they might not otherwise be able to communicate with.

Notice that I mentioned *community*. Allowing a spirit, even a God, to take possession of your faculties is a dangerous thing and you should have community to look after you. Preferably this community should be used to possession and have protocols and checks in place to ensure the safety of the possessed. There are all manner of things that a spirit might not think twice about but could potentially cause danger to the body of the possessed. Another reason for a community in matters such as dealing with the possessed is training to ensure the validity of the spirit. There are spirits who might say offensive things, perform lewd acts, or even physically assault people, but when a beloved spirit who has a relationship with a community does it, there is usually some wisdom conveyed or point demonstrated. Of course, there is also the possibility that a person *pretends* to be possessed so that they can get a pass on some shenanigans and blame them on spirits. It happens.

When Witches and Magicians say, "This is how magic is done in Vodoun and Shamanism," they are often focused on the dramatic and exoticized aspects of these practices, but ignore the roles that training and community play in this work. Because of this, I will not be covering it in this book.

That said, full possession does not occur every time a spirit and a person share a body and mind.

ASPECTING

The First Unitarian Church in Philadelphia was established in 1796. In 1886, the stone church that is still its home was constructed at 20th and Chestnut Street. It is the kind of place that not only welcomes people from all religions, but makes useful connections between them. In 1954, Martin Luther King, Jr. attended a lecture there on Mahatma Gandhi's nonviolent tactics in India. But in 1996 it was a hotspot for any fringe spiritual group that needed to rent some space in a suitably sacred environment.

The Spring Equinox that year saw me kneeling in my friend's linen robe in the church, meditating on Ra Hoor Khuit and chanting for about forty-five minutes before the ritual attendees were let in to the chamber. A small group of occultists had formed a cabal that met regularly and had submitted an application for our group, Thelesis, to become an encampment of the Ordo Templi Orientis. At some point during those preliminaries I could feel the presence of Horus. I had close-up visions of his hawk's face and could feel his scepter in my hand. I was definitely sharing space with something, but felt entirely in control. Until it was showtime.

Frater Koza let in the attendees, and Frater Xanthias performed the preliminary banishings. I remember getting up and seeing *a lot* of people there—way more than I expected. Apparently word got out that something weird was happening and people wanted to check it out. Perhaps it was Ra Hoor Khuit that got that ball rolling. I remember looking around and being momentarily stunned at the thirty or so people that had shown up. I vaguely remember what happened next, but it was not me doing it. I performed the Mass of the Phoenix, cutting a cross in my chest deeper than I wanted to, bleeding all over my friend's linen robe. I followed this with an invocation of Ra Hoor Khuit, based on Aleister Crowley's formula but tweaked a bit. With each utterance of "Thee I Invoke" I felt simultaneously more in control over my own body, yet also more connected to the God that I had invited in. I walked the semi-circle of guests, anointing them with oil and occasionally passing along words of wisdom from Horus. I remember thinking that some of what I was saying must be completely nonsensical, but after the fact, several people thanked me for the insight, so I guess Horus was on the money at least some of the time. At least when I was able to get out of his way.

The reason I am telling this story rather than just laying out terms is that this kind of manifestation of a spirit within you is a subtle and nuanced thing. There are a lot of shades of gray between full possession and a mere feeling of resonance or empowerment from the Deity, and I felt them all at different stages of this one ritual. At first it was like an essence pouring into me like water or a harmony with another being. If I got up at that point and played the role of God, as happens in most theatrical rituals that have assigned parts and scripted lines, it would have been an authentic magical experience, but lacking all the input from the actual spirit. After that, there was a state that started to move into full possession, where the Deity was doing most of the work, not just magical but muscular. This was followed by an equilibrium where I was sharing space and communicating while doing it.

TRANSVOCATION

There is a different state than the ones I previously mentioned that I call transvocation. In this state of manifestation the spirit is manifesting where you are physically, but you are also manifesting in the abode of that spirit. You are yourself and able to perceive the spirit as a presence, but you are also somehow inseparable. The spirit is in you and you are in them.

This is the neighborhood that Indian and Tibetan Tantra operates in, but it is not unique to those traditions. It is a mystical experience cultivated through long regular practices that last years. It is well worth the effort, but beyond the scope of this book.

For now, this wraps up the levels of manifestation.

WAIT! WHAT ABOUT DREAMS?

Dreams are actually the most common way for people to experience a spirit's contact, but it's tough to say where it falls in this scheme of manifestation. It depends on the dream. A dream is not so much defining the manifestation of the spirit as it is the lens you are perceiving that manifestation through.

Some dreams are simply sparked by spirit contact, and after that initial exposure your acetylcholine neurons just take that spark and run with it, creating God knows what. Maybe it's meaningful, maybe it's not, but you can say that about almost any kind of communication.

In other dreams, a spirit appears as asked and thus is a controlled appearance happening in the dream state rather than the waking state. Skilled dreamers can exploit the dream state very efficiently for this purpose, allowing a subtle being to manifest in a subtle state. There is a whole branch of yoga dedicated to this, which can yield visceral and consistent results. Training in Dream Yoga is beyond the scope of this book, but has been a huge benefit in my work with spirits. Also, I appreciate any yogic practice that encourages sleeping late.

Still, other dreams can be truly mystic experiences during which the spirit appears however it wishes, or even where you take on the role of the spirit in the dream. Whatever way a spirit manifests, you need the skills to make contact. So now that we know the ways that spirits can manifest, let's get some skills so that we can communicate when it happens.

CHAPTER 3

Spirit Skills

There are two types of people when it comes to spirits: those who are prone to psychic experiences and those who are not. Those who are not are often jealous of those who are, but they shouldn't be. *Both* types of people have work to do if they are going to successfully work with spirits, and the work of the person who is prone to easy psychic experiences is a bit harder.

We all know the first type of person. After the ritual or meditation group, they regale you with tales of the phantasmagoric experience they just had: Gods descending with messages of empowerment, mystic symbols, and maybe even messages for some of the other people in the circle. If you follow them online, somehow every God that they read about "shows up" or "calls upon them." I think we all know this person. If you don't know this person, it's possible that you *are* this person. That's okay, though. I was this person too. I had work to do.

This example is a bit extreme, but you get my meaning. Some people get into magic so they can experience spirits speaking to them, and others get into magic because they need to make the spirits shut up.

Those of us who are prone to psychic experience are at just as much a disability as those who aren't. It's just a different problem: if you close your eyes and see pictures or hear voices after every invocation, then you are getting a lot of fairly meaningless surface-level communication. What you need is a way to separate out the signal from the noise. What you need to do is improve your perception/projection ratio.

THE PERCEPTION/PROJECTION RATIO

Every experience you ever had is a mixture of your own perceptions of what actually happened, and the projections that you placed upon it. Not just spiritual experiences, *every experience*. Don't believe me? Call up a few friends that you had a memorable night with and go over in detail everything that happened.

This isn't just a trick of memory. Psychologists run experiments all the time that prove projections we place on the perception of things *we just saw* can be flawed or even flat-out wrong. If our perceptions of ordinary conversations and events are subject to this much distortion, how much more so are our spiritual experiences that are, by definition, even more subtle?

Thankfully the first tool that helps adjust your perception/projection ratio is just knowing that it exists. Knowing that some of what you experience with a spirit is probably a projection of your own mind is key to fine-tuning what the real message is. Sadly many people flatly reject this and have 100 percent faith that everything they think is a spirit actually is, and that they received and processed whatever came through correctly.

If you have an experience during which a spirit appears to you or gives a message to you, the most important thing you can do is ask yourself the following questions:

- Is this actionable?

- Is this useful?

Each of these questions can lead to other questions. Is it actionable? Is there any harm in taking the action? If a person I trusted or admired told me this, would I do it or believe it? Who will this benefit? Why is it good?

If the message is not actionable or useful, that doesn't mean you need to reject it as false. You don't need to do anything except make a note and keep doing what you're doing. This will prevent the gross ego inflation and self-important prattling that people sometimes get up to.

There is a Buddhist saying that goes: "If you see a Buddha on the road, kill him." Before you can know anything, you need to know your own mind, so if a God or a Buddha appears, it's not the time to drop what you are doing and go on a mental journey; it's time to keep meditating.

Which brings me to my next topic.

SIT DOWN AND SHUT UP

Anyone who has read my books or taken my courses is probably thinking "Oh no, he's gonna tell us to meditate, isn't he?"

Yes. Yes, I am.

Number one on the list of things I ask students to do, but which they usually don't do, is meditation. I get it. Meditation feels like the opposite of everything we get into magic for. We want to dance ecstatically and yell our conjurations; meditation says to sit still and be quiet. We want to have visions of the spirits and gods; meditation says to ignore those and tend to our own mind. We want excitement and a more magical life; meditation at the beginning stages is dull as dishwater.

The problem is that we only know things through the lens of our own mind. If we seek to know things that are so subtle that most people cannot perceive them, our lens needs to be clearer. Meditation is the best way I know for doing this.

You may have tried meditation and decided you are bad at it. Here's the thing: you *can't* be bad at it. Really. You can't be bad at it. People who think they are bad at meditation almost always misunderstand what is supposed to happen in meditation.

If you tried meditating and think you are bad at it, I can tell you what happened: you probably sat there, stared at the candle or watched your breath for a second or two, and had a thought. Then you returned to the breath or the candle for a couple more seconds and had another thought. Maybe a minute in you suddenly realized you not only had a thought, but you hadn't focused on the object of meditation for quite a while. Instead of the breath or the mantra, you were thinking about food or sex or whatever people think about when they are not thinking about food or sex. You chided yourself and got back into focus and then . . . it happened all over again. Rinse and repeat for the next twenty minutes until this interminably frustrating experience is over.

If that is a rough description of your meditation experience, I have good news for you: that is actually what is supposed to happen. You were meditating. Better yet, you were learning what your mind feels like when it is focused and recognizing when it is distracted. You were exercising the muscle that releases you from distraction and gets you back to what you have willed yourself to do. Even more important for our purposes: you were learning what your own thoughts and ideas feel like when examined. This is really vital if you plan to communicate with things that other people can't see or hear. These subtle voices, thoughts, and ideas that spirits communicate will require that clarity.

The good news is, I am going to make meditation very simple for you. Ready?

Sit down and shut up. Be still and silent for twenty minutes every day. If you can't do that, do ten minutes and work up from there. Any focus will do. Follow the breath. Stare at a flame or a point. Repeat a mantra. It doesn't matter. Sit some place you are comfortable and stable and focus your mind on that thing.

Isn't there more to it than that? Sure. There can be. You can learn about asanas to hold your body in, different ways to focus that might be better for you than others, different chants, or methods of releasing yourself from meditation. I teach a whole class on meditation called "Take Back Your Mind," and there are countless books, apps, and programs you can explore. But at the base, it is really about sitting down and shutting up for a bit. Do nothing and watch your mind.

One last thing: while you can't be bad at meditation, meditation practices can be bad for some people. It doesn't happen a lot, maybe half of one percent, but it is still worth talking about. There are some people who, when the pitter-patter of their usual thoughts slow down, experience traumatic memories or even get freaked out by a loss of Self. In some meditators, blood flows away from the parietal lobe that controls boundaries and toward the frontal lobe that controls analysis. You become hyper-aware of a loss of boundary. This is good for those looking to lessen the grasp of their ego, or for those looking to communicate with unseen intelligences, but it can be disruptive and traumatic for some. If something like this happens, consult relevant medical help. This is only a book, after all.

Suffice to say that 99 percent of you will not have any real difficulty with meditation beyond finding the discipline to do it. If you can, it is the one key that unlocks a thousand doors. You reach stages of sublime clarity and vastness far beyond those initial stages of recognizing distraction, but it takes work to get there. Even if you never get anywhere beyond recognizing distraction and releasing yourself from it, that will put you a step above most of humanity, and serve you well as you seek to consort with spirits.

JUST DO NOTHING

Yes, the act of sitting and doing nothing is actually a spirit skill. A vastly underrated one at that. When was the last time you did nothing? When was the last time you were bored? If you're like most people, it was probably a number of years ago before smart-phones. We have unwittingly robbed ourselves of something we didn't even know we needed: *idle time*. We cannot exercise without a podcast in our ears, we cannot wait in line without an app to distract us, we cannot eat a meal without taking a photo for Insta-gram. We are *never* bored, never idle.

"But wait a second, Jason! Didn't you just tell us to spend time meditating every day? Aren't we getting idle time through that?"

Meditation is not the same as idle time. If you are meditating, you are focused on one thing: the breath, an object, a mantra, and so on. When distractions arise, you release yourself from them and return to the focus of the meditation. You do this over and over and over again. There is nothing idle about that. Constant mental vigilance is the opposite of idle time. They may look the same from the outside, but from the inside they are utterly different.

For our purposes, idle time is an important skill to cultivate. Leaving the mind unoccupied allows for windows of clarity to appear amidst the normal patterns of thoughts and attachments.

Schedule walks or sessions of idle sitting, or get involved in repetitive tasks like mowing the lawn or gardening. Just let the mind go. Let it wander. Experience the fullness of your senses. Get used to relaxed noticing and mental play. It's important. Med-itation will sharpen your self-knowledge and help you know the content of your own mind, but idle time will give it license to just play. You imagine, you engage, you contemplate, you extrapolate.

Your idle time will cultivate your ability to open the senses, and it gives spirits the room to communicate with you. Your medi-tation time will give you the tool to go back over what you receive and separate out real communication from fantasy.

LOOK PAST THE VEIL

Not all spirit skills require discipline and training. Some are little tricks of perception that you can do anywhere at any time—even right now as you read this book. Try the following:

Step 1: Look straight ahead. It doesn't matter what is in front of you—anything from a sprawling vista to a wall will do. Just look.

Step 2: Now imagine that everything in front of you is actually on a video screen. Pretend it's a two-dimensional representation of what you see. It looks the same, just as it would if you were looking at a high-definition screen that took up your whole view, but you *know* that it is just a screen.

Step 3: Consider what is on the other side of that screen. Listen closely. Reach out with your feelings. Can you sense it? Is there something on the other side?

What this simple exercise does is collapse our normal sensation of three dimensions of space down to two dimensions, which leaves a mental "slot" open for us to perceive something we normally don't.

Warning: As simple as this exercise is, it has caused momentary nausea or dizziness in some students who try it. Others have been panicked by the sense of feeling beyond ordinary space, and the sensation that something might be looking back. As always, you have to monitor what you can and can't handle.

DREAMING TRUE

Perhaps the most prevalent and time-tested method of contact between humans and spirits is through dreams. What platform could be better for it? Every night your brain takes input you have received that day and makes images out of them. If a spirit was one of the things that you encountered that day in any way, then it has a chance to communicate via dream. How cool is that? It's like having a scrying mirror installed in our heads!

The beauty of this is that even if you lack psychic skills, a spirit will often be able to reach out to you in a dream after you have attempted to contact it. It's a platform switch. Sort of like saying, "Hey, I couldn't get through on the mobile, so I am gonna just leave this text here instead." No skills needed; you probably dream all the time.

Of course, just because you do something naturally doesn't mean that you can't do it *better*. There is a huge body of practice surrounding dreams, ranging from Greek lamps that encourage meaningful dreams to techniques of Dream Yoga that exploit the sleep state for spiritual growth.

There are two modes of dream work and each one has a different aim. The first attempts to cut through the meaningless drivel that dreams are often made of and encourage deeper, clearer, and more important dreams. Our conscious minds are passive during the reception of such dreams, simply taking in the message and hopefully remembering it long enough to jot it down when we wake up.

The second type of dream work revolves around the concept of lucid dreaming. In this type of work, rather than passively experience a dream, you wake up inside the dream and realize that it is, in fact, a dream. From this point we can take control of the experience and direct it however we wish: flying, inserting characters, transforming landscapes. You are in the dream with every other character and the environment in which the dream happens.

If we take control of the dream and change it, we are no longer experiencing whatever messages a spirit or the deep mind wants to convey, so for the purposes of spirit communication the focus should be on clearer dreams, improved recollection, and skillful interpretation. The work of lucid dreaming is important in other areas like mystical training and for learning Astral Projection (topics I have covered in courses, and may cover in a future book).

For now, the trick is to remember the dreams you have and attempt to get rid of the mental clutter that we generally construct dreams out of. If you watch *Jurassic Park* followed by the news right before bed, and you wind up having a dream about being chased by a Tyrannosaurus rex with Donald Trump's hair, it should not be hard to figure out where that imagery came from. Cutting through surface-level mind will allow deeper levels of your own mind, as well as communications from spirits, to come through.

If you are meditating, you are already doing the most important piece of this work! The clarity and mental self-possession you will build are the primary way to cut out that surface-level stuff. Here are a few other tips:

- No TV or reading right before bed. (Minimal input to disturb dreams.)

- Don't go to bed hungry. (Hunger disturbs sleep.)

- Keep the room dark. (A completely dark room increases melatonin, which aids in both sleep and dreams.)

- Wake and go back to bed. (Set your alarm a couple times through the night and write down what you were dreaming about. Since you only remember your most recent dreams, waking up several times a night will increase the options for what you remember.)

- Scents like rose, lavender, lilac, frankincense, and star anise have all been linked to improved dreams. (I have a covered bowl of star anise to smell before I do any serious dreaming work or scrying work.)

- Dietary supplements like melatonin and huperzine A can increase the vividness of dreams. (Consult your doctor before injesting anything.)

- Invoke and pray before bed.

One spell I have used is to draw, however crudely, an image of Hekate with two torches on one piece of linen and a key on another. Smoke them both in myrrh incense. Place the image of Hekate underneath you while you sleep, lengthwise under your spine, and the key image sideways under your pillow. Pray the following:

> Nebotousoaleth, Mistress of Movement in Dreams
> Let my key unlock the gates of the Onieros
> And allow (name of spirit) to appear and speak truthfully.
> May your twin torches burn behind my closed eyes
> And illuminate the corridors of sleep.
> IO HEKA IO HO.

PILLAR AND SPHERES

There is a ritual that I taught in my second book, *The Sorcerer's Secrets*, called the Pillar and Spheres, which arranges the five elements of Earth, Water, Fire, Air, and Spirit/Space on the body. This ritual is more than just a centering ritual. It doesn't simply introduce the elements and place them along the body so that they have a place to be—it arranges them in a particular pattern that encourages a subtle alchemy. Change the order of the elements and you will not get the same result.

In *The Sorcerer's Secrets* I gave some words for each point, but in this book I would love for you to simply breathe and focus on the element. For this ritual to *really* work, you have to know the qualities of the elements and let them release in the body. Aristotle described the four main elements according to a system of being wet or dry and hot or cold. Earth is dry and cool. Fire is hot and dry. Air is warm and wet. Water is cool and wet. There is a certain symmetry here where Fire and Water are opposites, as are Air and Earth. In addition to these qualities I would add qualities that speak to how these behave in their gross physical manifestations: Earth is stable, Fire consumes and expands, Water flows and fills, Air blows and moves rapidly.

When we do the Pillar and Spheres, we place Earth at the root not only because it is firm and solid, but because it gives the material that fire can consume. As we build the fire just below the navel, we consume the material below it and start heating everything above it. Water gets placed at the heart, which is brought to a boil by the fire below it. Steam rises from the water (remember Air is warm and wet according to Aristotle), which then melts the seed of Spirit/Space at the crown of the head. The wisdom of Spirit/Space then descends over the body, blessing each of the elements and making them even more potent and subtle. This is internal Alchemy: the rise of vitality and passion and the descent of ennobling wisdom.

The whole picture is rather like a Witch's cauldron inside the body. Earth is the ground and wood that the fire is built upon. The cauldron is set upon that fire and heats the water within it, releasing the cloud of steam and scent that rises to heaven.

What happens is that the entire body is sublimated and made more subtle, more spirit like. Those who want to take this to the extreme can research Tummo or internal heat practices, which turn up the volume on this process through intense breathing and muscle manipulations. I wrote my own instructions for this in my book *Sex, Sorcery, and Spirit,* and there you can read a traditional Tibetan instruction in the Bliss of Inner Fire by Lama Yeshe. It is a rather complicated process so I am not including it here. If you master the Pillar and Spheres and want to take it further, you know where to go.

SO MUCH MORE . . .

There are so many exercises, techniques, and trainings available that I can't possibly go over all of them. This is to get you started on your journey and to get you to think about your own capacity for sensing spirits as something that is not merely a gift, but as a skill that can be learned and improved upon. When you are actually in the field trying to contact a spirit in the woods or the graveyard, or summoning a Demon into the Temple, you now know that it's not simply a matter of a spirit revealing itself. It's also about your ability to perceive that spirit when it does.

So start here, but explore all your options. The methods of pushing past our ordinary senses are far too numerous to name here, but most of them can help you in this work.

THE MOST IMPORTANT SKILL TO MASTER

One more thing, and this is *crucial*. Whether you are completely new to this, or have been chatting with spirits for years, you *must* cultivate a healthy dynamic tension between allowing the play of awareness to run free and critically analyzing your experiences.

Sadly, it's the one thing that most people involved in Witchcraft and the occult lack, and people fall into the clutches of either extreme doubt or unquestioning acceptance. If you start to doubt everything that you perceive, you won't be able to engage it enough to cultivate more. However, if you start to believe whole-heartedly that every brain fart and fantasy that pass through your head are an important message from the spirits, you are gonna spin your wheels and go nowehere. The rule is this:

Engage the experience without doubt while it is happen-ing. Analyze it critically after it is over.

To experience something outside the normal, you have to be open to it. You must learn to let the mind play. Engage in a bit of imagination. Let daydreaming run wild. If you just called out to a spirit, either in ritual or while walking in the woods, let your mind go and whatever happens *roll with it*. You are trying to expe-rience something that is quite subtle. Something that you already know is going to be part perception and part projection. If you get hypercritical while it is happening, it won't happen. It's like worrying too much about whether you are really balanced while riding a bike—if you don't let go, you simply won't get that bal-ance. You can't force everything to adhere to the ordinary senses, because those are the very senses that you are trying to transcend! Give yourself some slack.

If a spirit appears and speaks, just accept it. Stop worrying about whether it's your own imagination or not. A huge number of students who tell me they can't perceive spirits actually *do* have experiences. They just instantly dismiss them as fantasy.

After the communication is over, *now* it's time to be critical about your experience. I mean really ruthless. Put your experience through a checklist:

- Was there anything actionable that I got out of this?

- Does taking those actions make sense, or at least cause no harm?

- Did I learn anything verifiable?

- Was the spirit or vision something that strokes my ego, or was it challenging?

Let me tell you that 60 to 80 percent of what I get from spirits does *not* pass this gauntlet of questions with flying colors. That's okay; human beings don't fare that much better. It is way less important to obsess over whether a message is really from Hekate or Diana or the ghost around the corner than it is to consider the content of the message itself. If the message is actionable or informative and those actions and information prove useful, that is more important than where it comes from. If, however, the information is just ego-stroking, then it doesn't matter much. "Jason! I am the creator God Arceus, go forth and preach my message which is: Gotta Catch 'Em Now!" is not something I would find worth investing time in, even if Arceus *did* deliver it.

If you can manage to cultivate both a mind that can manage critical evaluation *and* engagement of the imagination, you will be well equipped to consort with the spirits.

CHAPTER 4

Respect and Authority

Before we dig in to this chapter, I want you to take a moment and think about the people in your life you would listen to and why. Let's say you need love advice. If your friend who has the same track record as you offers it, you may heed it or you may not, but you will surely hear them out because they are a friend with similar experience. If it's someone who has been happily married for a long time, especially someone a bit older than you, you probably should listen more intently because they have achieved what you are hoping to achieve. If the person was too much older, you might feel they are out of touch with your situation and disregard their opinion. If a stranger overhears your conversation and offers the advice, you might be annoyed and just ignore them or nod politely. If you paid money for someone to help you, then I am sure you would pay close attention because they are a professional. If it's your significant other telling you what they need, then you *better* listen or else. . . .

This all might be the same bit of advice but it could be taken different ways. Why? Because of the respect you have for the person giving it. That relationship with the spirits needs to be established, or there can be no meaningful exchange. If you have no respect for the spirits, then why bother trying to make contact? If they have no respect for you, why would they listen?

The theme of this chapter is "Just Like with People . . ."

EARN RESPECT

As I mentioned in Chapter 2, the first time I ever summoned a spirit it was the Demon Astaroth. I was young and the spirit was listed as one of the rulers of the Americas in the *Grimoire Verum*. Since I lived in America, it seemed like a handy spirit to know. I set about doing it as best as my sixteen-year-old self could manage. This involved a "temple" that consisted of my bedroom floor cleared of all laundry and garbage (sixteen-year-old boys tend to be gross and I was no exception), and an "altar" that was actually an old end table that my mom was throwing out. Sadly there were not a lot of great copies of the *Grimoire Verum* floating around in 1987, so I was working from *The Complete Book of Magic and Witchcraft* by Kathryn Paulsen. Much to my surprise, it worked! But *why* did it work? The setup was laughable and the text I was working with was incomplete. There are two factors that I think contributed to my success:

First, even though I was working with an incomplete text, the main words of summoning were there—words that have been spoken before. Words that another Magician summoned her with and either got her to willingly agree to answer or made her forcibly bound to do so. I think in this case it was the former. So that was the first factor. I was standing on the shoulders of giants and using protocols that had already been set up for contacting this Astaroth.

Second, I had spent the previous year and a half performing rituals from Donald Kraig's Modern Magick program. It's not on the top of my list for students today, but in 1987 it was a game-changer. It gave me a serious daily practice that was workable and well explained. Every day I was calling divine light into my

Consorting with Spirits

body and activating key points in the middle pillar ritual, invoking Archangels to stand at the quarters of my temple and bless me in the Lesser Banishing Ritual of the Pentagram, orienting myself to the royal stars in the Hexagram ritual, meditating, and a host of other magics. This is not the daily regimen I would recommend to people now, but Magicians who hold *any* serious daily regimen are often leaps and bounds ahead of those who don't. This all aided me not only in being able to make contact with our Demon Queen of the Americas, but helped me be worthy of being noticed. Just like with people, it's not just the words spoken, but who spoke them.

So that's how I got my initial meeting. But just like with people, that first meeting only gets your foot in the door. What you build from that point is on you. I decided that even though many texts seem to indicate that Demons needed to be strictly bound, this was a bit too aggressive and imperialist for me. I opted to go the route of offerings and mutual service and build my relationship with her that way. I saw myself more as a Witch who worked ceremonial magic than a classic Ceremonial Magician. In my mind, Witches got on with Demons more than bossed them around. I am glad I did because she has been a good ally for more than thirty years now.

Of course, there are other ways to establish respect and build relationships. More forceful ways, that is.

EXERCISE AUTHORITY

In the late 1990s I got interested in following grimoires as close as I could to the letter. Though different books give different formulas, there is no assumption of magical training for the operator. Meditation and energy work did not figure into the lives of most grimoire writers. Instead, the exorcist undergoes a period of purification that entails intense prayer, fasting, and abstinence. The evocations in these manuals closely follow the patterns of Catholic exorcisms.

In this scenario, the spirit is called to appear, *or else*. Just like with an exorcism, if the spirit does not obey, the spirit is punished. Some grimoires tell you to roast the seal of the spirit over hot coals to get him to appear. This may sound extreme, but there are reasons for it. There are some spirits who will only respond to force, and some who need to be motivated by force to accomplish what you have set out for them to do. There is also the idea that once you start something this forceful, you can't stop until it's done. If you have ever been in a fight, you know what I mean: you can't just decide halfway through to drop it and be friends because that person is gonna take the opening and break your nose. I speak from experience.

Forceful authority is also used to get a spirit to appear in the specific mode of manifestation you want. A spirit who might be comfortable supplying loose inspirations or hazy manifestations of resonance when asked might only be motivated to appear visibly and speak plainly when compelled to controlled appearance. Some people are like this too, only giving straight answers when under a penalty of violence or imprisonment.

We can see that forceful methods are not just a matter of Magicians resorting to drastic means for no reason; it is a matter of making a spirit orient itself in a way that the Magician can question it and understand it clearly. Magicians who do not put any work into spirit skills that enable them to more readily perceive subtler layers of reality will need these methods to have any kind of communication at all. Some authors like the late Joseph Lisiewski would insist that it's not even safe to communicate with a spirit until it is constrained and appearing visible and clear. I don't buy into that as an overall rule for spirits, but it's something to keep in mind in some sticky situations.

I live by the philosophy articulated by Theodore Roosevelt: "Speak softly and carry a big stick." When it comes to spirits, I want to have cordial relationships, and I do not need every spirit I work with to orient itself as close to the physical as possible. That said, I also need to know that I *can* compel a spirit when I need to.

If you cannot compel a spirit, then you can't exorcise one either, in which case, it's dangerous to start inviting spirits into your life.

This is not fear of spirits, or a bossy attitude. It is the same with people. You might think twice about inviting a new neighbor over for tea if you could not defend yourself or had no way to call the police should things get out of hand. It really is that simple.

My rule is: Don't be needlessly aggressive with spirits, but be prepared to exercise authority, and occasionally force, when you need to.

How does one gain spiritual authority? There are numerous ways.

Conferred Authority

"Membership has its privileges." This was the tagline of a popular commercial for American Express, but it's also applicable for the type of spiritual authority conferred upon you by belonging to a priesthood, cabal, order, or other group.

In the physical world, a police officer's authority is conferred by being hired into a police force that holds respect and power in the community. Membership has its privileges. Members of priesthoods and magical orders also have privileges, and depending upon the group, they carry a certain level of spiritual authority.

When Tibetan Buddhists invoke the aid of fierce Dharmapalas like Rahula of Ekajati, they first need to call upon a great Magician like Padmasambhava, who actually bound those spirits to serve initiated Tantrikas that would follow in his lineage. It is that conferred authority that makes the practice both safe and effective.

When a priest performs an exorcism, he is doing it based upon the Holy Orders he received, which carry the spiritual authority that has been passed down all the way back from the original Apostles. Most of the grimoires that give seals and conjurations for calling Demons are likely written for people who have been consecrated at least through the minor orders: the last of which is "Exorcist."

Various African traditional religions and Afro-Caribbean religions also confer spiritual authority for dealing with the powers invoked in those rituals. This is just one reason why members of those religions get upset when people claim to be Voodoo priests, santeros, or paleros based on the books that they have read. There is something that cannot be conferred by reading. Some people claim to receive initiations from the spirits, but if you use that claim to make it seem like you were initiated into a priesthood or order that is normally conferred by people, be prepared to be called out for misappropriation and lies rather than being welcomed with open arms.

None of this is to say that conferred authority is necessary for working with spirits generally. Tibetans will sometimes pray to a Dharmapala even if they are not initiated Tantrics, but they are not binding them or making strong demands as they would in a Tantric ceremony. Most Afro-Caribbean religions are community based, and so non-initiates pray to Iwa and Orisha all the time, but they don't call themselves houngans or tatas, and they don't have access to the same ceremonies. Magicians who do not hold Holy Orders summon spirits from the grimoires all the time, but they do it on a different basis than a priest or bishop would.

Of course some spirits will *only* ever answer to initiates. That is their role: to serve or interact with a closed group of devotees or initiates. Violate that pact at your own risk.

That said, what a group *claims* to have access to and what they *actually* have access to are different things. Some Christians or Buddhists will say that any spirit will bow down to the powers of their religion because of its inherent power. Maybe, maybe not. Other groups will claim that certain spirits are only available to people of certain ethnicities, ancestral lines, or initiations. Maybe, maybe not. I cannot sort that out for you. All I can say is look for evidence of claims. If a group tells you that its spirits confer amazing wealth and power, but everyone in that group has ordinary jobs and struggles, then maybe it's, in the words of Joe Biden, a bunch of malarky.

Invoked Authority

"I am Moses your prophet to whom you have transmitted your mysteries celebrated by Israel. You have revealed the moist and the dry and all nourishment. Hear me! I am the messenger of Pharaoh Osorronophris. This is your true name which has been handed down to the prophets of Israel. Hear me! ARBATHIAŌ REIBET ATHELEBERSĒTH ARA BLATHA ALBEU EBENPHKHI KHITASGOĒ IB AŌTH IAŌ"

These words were written some 1,800 years ago on a papyrus, which was kept hidden for centuries before being unearthed by archaeologists, translated into English, then spoken again by Magicians looking to summon or banish spirits.

I can remember the first time I ever attempted it. I was doing the version of it that passed through Aleister Crowley and is known as Liber Samekh. Crowley included it in his copy of the *Goetia of Solomon* as a preliminary. As I spoke the words, I kept waiting for a spirit to laugh and say, "Uhhhhh dude, you are *not* Moses," but none did.

The ritual is easily the most famous of the papyri graecae magicae (PGM) spells. It establishes you as Moses, which makes you worthy to summon the Headless God (in Aleister Crowley and Golden Dawn [GD] texts they mistranslate this as "bornless"), who you then charge to "make all Spirits subject unto Me: so that every Spirit of the Firmament and of the Ether: upon the Earth and under the Earth: on dry Land and in the Water: of Whirling Air, and of rushing Fire: and every Spell and Scourge of God may be obedient unto Me." I'm sure you can see why that would be an attractive precurser to summoning Demons.

This is an example of invoked authority. You haven't had anyone confer authority on you permanently as a matter of initiation or ordination. You are, however, invoking the names of powerful Gods or Magicians from the past who will compel a spirit to obey. In this case, the reason you identify with Moses is that he is both a giver of Divine Law and a guy whose magic was proven greater than that of pharaoh's greatest Magicians. You want the spirits to believe that you *are* Moses. You need to act accordingly.

Modern Pagans adopt God forms in a similar way: they see themselves as the Deity, they invoke the Deity, and in some small way they become the Deity (at least long enough to work some magic). I told you a story earlier in the book where I did the same with Horus.

Of course, you don't always pretend to *be* someone else to hold authority. You can simply invoke their names, qualities, and powers. Not just the top guy either, but a hierarchy that extends all the way down to the spirit just above who you are calling. In a Christian context this might include the Trinity, the Virgin Mary, certain relevant saints, then spirit kings of the earth, rulers of hell, along with infernal presidents, dukes, and so on. A good part of the grimoires is literally the "org chart from hell."

If someone devoted to Hekate wanted to achieve the same thing, they might spend time invoking Hekate by her various names and epitaphs, then call spirits associated with her such as Lampads, Gorgons, and such. One could even call upon various Hekatean "saints" such as Medea or Circe. With the endorsement of these powers, the spirits you want to call will listen and behave not necessarily because you are calling them, but because of *whom* you have successfully called upon in order to contact them.

I would encourage you to construct something like this for whatever powers you are most dedicated to and have spent the most time with. See, the reason these names work to compel spirits is not just the respect the name commands in the spirit world, nor the faith you have in the name. It's also the investment that power has in *you*. Go ahead and think about all the magic you have done before reading this book and put together an invocation that calls other spirits by those names.

Earned Authority

When Christ performed exorcisms, one of the things that got him in trouble was that he didn't do it in any name but his own. Since he was not using any of the names of God that Demons would normally be commanded by, the scribes accused him of commanding demons in the name of Beelzebub. Now, if you are a devout Christian, you believe that Christ commanded Demons in his own name because he *was* God. It is worth noting, however, that the first written description of Christ is on a bowl that calls him a goistas,[1] a Sorcerer.

I believe that you can become a person who wields innate authority—not granted by outside powers, or invoked through ritual means, but simply wielded because you are a being of power. You are a spirit too, after all. We are all Buddhas or Gods in potential.

How you accomplish this is a matter of debate, though it is thought that people who attain a deep knowing through meditation or who learn to channel spiritual forces through their body achieve such states. This realization takes a long time. All over the world great mystics spend time in retreat getting to know their own mind and spirit. Yogis and yoginis learn to control the powers of the body to an extent that it unlocks their divine potential. The fruit of such work creates an innate authority that is respected as much or more than any other type of authority. You do not have to be particularly realized or advanced; simply being on this path confers a certain level of respect from the spirits.

THE LONELY INITIATION

There is another method of earned authority that doesn't take years of work and practice. It is usually a single experience that lasts a few moments to a few hours. You come out the other side a different being than who you were going in. Robin Artisson calls this becoming "Witched," a term I wish I'd thought to use first because it's so accurate and good.

How does this happen? I can't really lay it all out for certain. This initiation is not a script you follow where you get challenged by people playing prescribed roles at four quarters of the circle. If someone holds a sword to your throat during one of those affairs, you can bet they won't actually cut you if you get it wrong. Someone will whisper the answer and let you continue playing your part. These are useful initiatory ceremonies for sure, but in the Lonely Initiation, if there is nothing real on the line, it doesn't happen.

So how does it start? Going somewhere dark and doing something forbidden at a special time usually will get the ball rolling. In Sweden, a career in Magic is sometimes started by undertaking the Årsgång, or year's walk. In this practice you walk around a church on Christmas Eve, sometimes backward, and encounter the devil or another spirit who might issue a challenge. Only after doing this will you have the power to work the spells in a Svartkonst-böcker, Black Books of magic often connected with St Cyprian.

My obeah mentor Christopher Bradford instructed me to spend the night in the forest in a particular state that will bring you into contact with a being who initiates. In other traditions it's a psychedelic mixture that sends you on your way. I am not a huge fan of chemical-induced magic, but I would be lying if I didn't say that a powerful "flying ointment" and a night in the woods were not involved in one of the most life-changing events I ever had.

In the United States, blues musicians talk about going to the crossroads at dawn to meet the devil and learn to play guitar. The feature of the crossroads is almost universal, and also plays a role in Swedish magic. The most famous Witch in Sweden, Märet Jonsdotter, was said to take young women to a three-way crossroads where the devil would show himself dressed as a vicar and share a meal with them.

Sometimes people undergo the Lonely Initiation while on pilgrimage. This happened to me in Pashupatinath, where I sat for three days meditating on impermanence at the cremation ground. Sometimes people undergo it during near-fatal illnesses. This is what happened to celebrated spiritualist and fellow Vermonter Achsa W. Sprague who almost died of rheumatic fever, but was able to communicate with spirits after she was healed.

In the end, even if someone is there to help you get started, the Lonely Initiation is between you and the spirits. It can happen more than once in a lifetime, and each time will affect you in different ways. There is no script, no way to control what happens, nor any way to ensure it happens at all.

What I can tell you is that if it happens, you won't need to run out and tell the world about this. It will change you and people will notice, as will spirits. That is the *only* worth that such an experience has. If you try to use it to claim part in a club, or as a badge of authority that should not be questioned, you will just look like a fool. You get no bragging rights from the Lonely Initiation. Let your actions and behavior speak of your status.

MUTUAL RESPECT

The previous examples are of *Authority*. As I said earlier, I think it's very handy to wield some kind of authority in life. When you *need* it, nothing replaces it. In many situations, some kind of established mutual respect will get you further than asserting your authority.

Think about it: when you are compelled to do something, are you excited for the work or do you do the bare minimum just to not suffer consequences? That's how I get. However, when someone I respect asks me for something, I do my very best for them. If it is friends and family, I want to exceed expectations out of love. If it is someone I admire, I want to exceed expectations in order to impress them. Forging a relationship from respect rather than authority is almost always preferable.

Offerings are the best way I can think of to start building relationships on the basis of mutual respect. If a stranger came up to you and asked for $100, you would probably say no, right? You don't know this person or have any history with this person. If, however, a coworker asked you for $100, you might say yes, or you might say no. It depends on your relationship. Have you gone out to lunch dozens of times? Do they ever pay for you on occasion? If they treat you, do you treat them occasionally? Even if it's not totally even every time, do you trust that it all evens out in the end? If so, you probably trust them enough to loan the money. If, however, they have shown themselves to be miserly at these times, you probably won't. This is how people test each other's trust and reliability. Over time, confidence builds between parties.

It's the same thing with regular offerings. You start to make offerings to the local beings, to your allies, to your gods, and even to beings you might have pissed off, and you start to build a relationship where beings are willing to help you out—not because they have to, but because they want to.

THE SPIRIT FEAST

I have taught the following ritual for almost twenty years now. Students who undertake it on a regular basis often report back that it has been one of the biggest game-changers in their magic. It's deceptively simple. All you need is some incense and a libation such as wine, tea, coffee, or water. You can add more if you want, and perhaps the spirits will make suggestions as you progress in this practice, but for now keep things simple.

Step 1: Purification

In this step you purify your offerings, marking them as special and no longer ordinary material. Lay out your incense, libation, and any other items that you plan on offering. Lay your hands over them in a gesture of blessing. The following words and visualizations will purify these offerings and make them both desirable and accessible to the spirits.

Make a gesture of consecration over the offerings:

Fire of Fire, First of the Fire within me,
Burn away the impurities of the offering

Visualize the offerings on fire and consider that this consumes any impurity in the offering substances and consecrates them by fire.

Air of Air, first of the Air within me,
Extinguish the fire and separate the ash from offering

Visualize a wind that blows out the fire and consecrates the offerings by air.

Water of Water, first of the Water within me,
Cleanse this offering so that only subtle substance
    remains.

Visualize a torrent of water that passes over and through the offerings, washing away the ash from the extinguished fire and consecrating the offerings by water.

Earth of Earth, first of the Earth within me,
Multiply this offering that this sole support may fill the
    ten directions and satisfy all who seek sustenance

Visualize the offerings multiplying and filling all of the space.

Spirit of Spirit, first of the Spirit within me,
Transform this offering into whatever is most desire-
    able that it may please the six doors of sensation and
    delight my honored guests

Consider that the offerings take the pattern of whatever the recipient finds most pleasing.

Step 2: Invite the Guests

Now that your offerings are purified, you need to invite all the guests that you want to extend this offering to. This ritual is not a targeted offering to one spirit, or even a single group of spirits. It is aimed widely, at four classes of being:

Deities or Enlightened Beings: That which you con-
    sider the most high.

Guardians and Allies: Powerful beings whom you have special relationships with, such as Angels, Demons, Dharmapalas, and so on.

Local beings: This starts with the spirits of your local area and the beings of the underworld, land, and sky where you are performing this. From there it can extend to the town, state, country, and so on. A Sorcerer with a big enough view would encompass the whole world.

Beings you owe a debt to: We can upset some spirits, especially nature spirits, through our ordinary modes of human living. As Witches and Magicians, we can also do things that have unintentional impacts on a spirit and subtle ecology more directly. This part of the offering is a way of acknowledging this and making some small amends.

To the Gods and Goddesses,
Angels and Avatars
arch devils and glorified dead
most especially to (name your most important patrons
    and divine beings that you wish to acknowledge by
    name)
And to the overseeing powers of this land on which I
    dwell
I give offerings of respect
to the Ancestors, Guardians, Familiars, saints, and potent
    allies I give thanks and offering
most especially (name your most important ancestors,
    protectors, and spirit allies that you wish to acknowl-
    edge by name)
I give offerings of gratitude
to all beings of the sky, the land, the underworld.
To all sentient beings in all the ten directions and three
    times

to beings of the elements, and all who wander the surface
    of the earth
I give offerings of substance and nourishment
to all beings to whom I owe a debt, and whom I have
    angered by mistaken or ignorant action
I give offerings of supplication and pacification.

Step 3: Give the Offerings

Make the gesture of offering, flourish your incense, pour your
libation on the ground, hold aloft your light, set out your cups of
alcohol. Do whatever you do as a signature of offering—truth be
told, it doesn't matter. It is a signal to the spirits that the offering
is made. Imagine that the offerings are multiplied.

Let the offerings arise and pervade all space
let it take the form that is most desired
Enjoy! Enjoy!
friends and family from former lives
I am grateful for your past kindness
Enjoy! Enjoy!
you who form obstacles as retribution to my action
forgive any offense made by mistake or delusion
Enjoy! Enjoy!
spirits of the dead and trapped in-between spaces
wardens of this ground and keepers of the winds
Enjoy! Enjoy!
guardians and familiars, be fullfilled
thank you for your aid
Enjoy! Enjoy!
to each of you I offer inexhaustable treasures
delightful substances and enjoyments.
You who would harm me,
partake of this feast and be at peace
you who would help me be fullfilled
so it is.

Add in your own visualization of the offerings multiplying and filling all space. Spend some time looking at what the spirits do with the clouds and how they manifest.

> Enjoy the offerings
> be pleased and fulfilled.
> License to depart
> When you leave, bow in respect just as you would if you
>   left a party.
> Honored guests of this temple, the window of our com-
>   munion is closing and our feast is coming to an end.
> Take your last taste of these enjoyments and go in peace.
> Vacate the thrones of the feast and go forth unto your
>   abodes and habitations as you desire
> forever act as friends and helpers
> accomplish all the deeds with which you have been
>   charged
> by the power of the hand and eye
> and the arcana of the sacred arte
> so mote it be

Simple enough, right? Give it a try. There are ways of making it longer for a large ceremony, and ways of making it shorter for when you are pinched for time. I do this, or a variation of it, every day. If you do it, things will start to show up. If you work on the skills from the last chapter, you can perceive them and communicate with them.

This is one path to consorting with spirits that uses a relationship based on mutual respect through regular offerings.

CHAPTER 5

Prayers and Spells

I saw the lights flashing in the rearview mirror and that feeling of mild dread and annoyance came over me. I pulled over hoping that the officer was going to speed past to some emergency, but he pulled up behind me on the side of the road. Apparently, I failed to notice that the speed limit dropped from 45 to 25 miles per hour. I immediately envisioned Hekate in the mind, and said a short invocation to her. The officer came to the car window, told me I had been speeding, and collected my driver's license and registration. As he left, I began chanting a mantra to Hekate: IO HEKA IO HO and envisioned it leaving my mouth and entering the officer's nose, circulating through his body, and then back to me. After about twenty-one repetitions I stopped and made a short request for the officer to let me go with minimal fuss and no ticket. He handed back my documents and told me he would let me off with a warning. He drove away and I thanked Hekate for her swift intercession. When I got home, I made a special offering to her, as well as to local spirits she works through.

In this example, I did not receive any messages from Hekate. No communications from her of any kind were required. I spoke a prayer, visualized a bit, and then stated what I wanted to occur. It was a request for assistance. The only answer back was the fact that it worked.

Whether it's your grandmother asking St. Anthony to find her car keys ("Tony, Tony, look around. Something's lost and must be found!") or an ancient Sorceress carving a curse tablet in lead dedicated to Hekate and then burying it at a three-way crossroads (where the underworld mail system will pick it up and deliver the message), it's the same basic pattern. This is how spirits are interacted with most of the time. No great skill is needed to discern the voice of the Gods, nor any oracle to divine their assistance. Communication happens one way, and then whatever happens, happens.

Now, this is a book about consorting with spirits, not a book of prayers or spells. Books with prayers and spells exist in abundance, so why cover this? Two reasons: first, one-way communication is still communication, so it would just be sloppy not to say something about interacting with spirits in this way. So many people feel they have a close relationship with a God or a spirit based solely on their prayer life that you really can't ignore it. I know a circle of old Catholic ladies who are very clearly favored by spirits and saints that they pray to. Their requests move and shake their community, even though they never claim to receive any communication back from the spirits. Are they Witches? Not for me to decide, but for my money they are.

The other reason is that if you do cultivate a strong relationship with Gods and spirits, your prayers and spells will have a higher success rate. It was no coincidence that I chose Hekate to ensorcell the police officer who pulled me over. I have a regular practice that I keep up and I lead hundreds of people a year through a training program dedicated to her. When I pray or do a spell, she tends to answer because I have this good relationship.

FROM PRAYER TO SPELL

Intercession is not the only type of prayer. There are prayers of thanksgiving, adoration, praise, lamentation, and simple union, but when it comes to magic, it's those prayers for intercession that grab the spotlight.

Is a prayer the same as a spell? Some say yes, and I won't argue with them. Prayer is certainly a factor in many, if not most spells. Other people would say that a spell is more than just a prayer and that it requires something more, like an act of sympathetic magic, or the mantra and visualization given on page 71. There is also the matter of expectation. A pious prayer leaves it up to the Gods, "thy will be done" and all that, whereas a good spell is expected to actually produce results.

Prayers and spells have one thing in common: there is no expectation that the God or spirit will answer back directly right then. Other than the requested change, this is one-way communication. Since I brought up Hekate, try this on for size:

A Prayer to Hekate to Open the Gates of Spirit

Hail many named mother of the gods, whose children
    are fair
Hail mighty Hekate of the threshold, keyholder of the
    world
Hail to enodia, keeper of the four- and three-way cross-
    roads
Nether, nocturnal and infernal one
I beckon to you, hear my plea
Night mother! Savior! Mistress of solitude!
Lady of light, and the darkness that contains it
You who walk disheveled and wild through tombs and
    cremation grounds
Cloaked in saffron, crowned with oak leaves and coils of
    serpents
You who are followed by hordes of ghosts, dogs, and
    restless spirits

Yet are also the luminous empress of the empyrian
    realms.
I beckon to you, hear my plea
Kleidokhous, grant me the key to the mysteries
Propylaia, throw open the gateway to the world of spirits
Phosphoros, light my way with your twin torches of
    mercy and severity
Propolos, steer me safely through the four rivers of spirit
Brimo, shake the pillars of perception with your wrath
Physis, bind all Demons and troublemaking spirits
Kleidokhous, grant me the key to the mysteries
Anassa eneroi, queen of the dead, bring me contact
With my Ancestors and the shades of Witches past.
Hekate Chthonia, Queen of Sorcery
Teacher of howlings and bindings, curses and blessings
Bring to me all spirits I call in your name
Whether they be dwelling in the earth or the underworld
In the swirling airs or highest heavens
In the fires or waters of anyplace anywhere
Bring them forth and grant me their conversation.

It's a simple prayer asking for Hekate to aid you in opening
your senses to the spirits, and for her to aid you in bringing spirits
you call. Prayers are potent, and if you repeat it regularly, it will
slowly change you. It doesn't do all the work for you, but if you
train your senses and make regular offerings, this rite will be a
catalyst for your work. If you don't, then there is nothing for it to
catalyze.

Now, let's say you do this prayer in front of a statue or a visualization of Hekate. You cap it off with an offering of incense, or
maybe nicely arranged eggs, honey, and some dandelions. Now
you have something slightly more than a prayer. Is a prayer with
this additional focus and offering a spell?

Let's add some more. After the prayer, spend some time meditating on her, and chant to her: IO HEKA IO HO over and over

again. This is a chant that she gave me in my first working with her. IO is an opening of invocations for many Greek and Roman Deities. HEKA is not just related to her name, but means "beyond," as in stretching your own senses beyond the norm. IO HO is the finalizing syllables that set it in motion.

Let this mantra lead you into a trance, and then when you stop chanting, listen. What can you hear or sense? Reach out with your senses.

What started as a prayer is now a full-blown exercise. But maybe you don't think this is magic either. For some people magic is less in the head and more in the hand.

Perhaps you might want to make a talisman to help aid you in your efforts with spirits. On the night of a dark moon, take a small leather bag with star anise, mugwort, dandelion, angelica, wormwood, adder's tongue, and a small stone from a river that has a hole worn in it, otherwise known as a holy stone. Tie a thread with eleven knots through the holy stone and place it in the bag with the herbs. Say the prayer and ask Hekate to lay her hands upon the amulet so that it may facilitate your travels and trafficking between worlds. Chant the IO HEKA chant on the knots, letting them lead you to the hole in the stone: a symbol of the gate between spirit and matter. Breathe the mantra into it. Close the bag and only open it on dark moons to recharge the bag with more offerings and chants. Pass the bag three times through a candle flame, and now our simple prayer is the base of a spell.

Of course, we need not only limit our prayers and spells to Gods. There is a long tradition of appealing to saints and powerful Magicians of the past as intercessors.

THE SORCERER'S CALL TO ST CYPRIAN

Sorcerers are a funny bunch. Since we are concerned with the reality of the spirits themselves rather than adhering to one religious view or another, you might find us doing a rite to Hekate

Consorting with Spirits

one hour and appealing to a Christian saint the next. My favorite saint for consorting with spirits is St Cyprian of Antioch.

This 4th century hieromartyr was the most learned and famous Sorcerer of his time, having trained in magic and Necromancy all over the Mediterranean world. The story is that he set his eyes on a beautiful maiden named Justina, and used his magic to try to win her love. Much to her Pagan parents' chagrin, Justina was a devout Christian, and when she felt the onslaught of Cyprian's Demons, she dispelled them with the sign of the cross. He of course sent more Demons. She swatted them away like flies with the cross again. He consulted Lucifer and sent the most powerful Demons he could find, and she sent them packing with the sign of the cross. Impressed by this display of power, he converted to Christianity, eventually becoming a bishop. She became a nun and they became close friends. Eventually they were martyred together in 304 during the Diocletianic Persecution. For Christians, that's the end of the story. For Witches, Sorcerers, and Magicians, it's just the start.

While Christians claim he was moved by Christianity to renounce his occult practices, there are other versions of the story. In these versions, Cyprian did not renounce Sorcery, but instead practiced it in secret, right alongside his Christian duties. In a world filled with Gods and spirits, Christianity represented just another set of powers one could appeal to and align with. Some say that he and Justina carried on a magical partnership like Simon Magus and Helena had done before them. Some legends say that Cyprian recorded his occult knowledge in a secret spell book— one of the most powerful in the world. There have since been many books claiming either to be Cyprian's or to be inspired by his occult wisdom. Though not as well known in English-speaking countries until recently, from Norway to Iberia to Brazil the term "Cyprianus" is a euphemism for a magical book.

In Spain, Portugal, Mexico, and Brazil, Cyprian is a very popular saint not only because of the magic he taught, but as a power to appeal to directly. Statues, spell kits, lithographs, oils, and soaps concerning the saint are sold in botanicas for those seeking occult wisdom along with dozens of different versions of spell books claiming connection to him. A lot of information on this magnificent saint is available in English thanks to the efforts of scholars like José Leitão and Humberto Maggi who made the first English translations of Cyprian spellbooks.

I became obsessed with the saint after receiving a Peruvian vial amulet that contained an image of him back in 2004. After many years of research and conjuration, I wrote the following prayer that has now been used by Sorcerers all over the world.

The Sorcerer's Call to St Cyprian

In the name of the great and mighty power of God I invoke the sublime influence of St. Cyprian, in Christ Jesus. I ask that you be my mentor and my master by virtue of the grace bestowed upon you by God omnipotent who was, who is, and who will ever be.

You learned to control storms on Mt. Olympus, the casting of enchantment and illusion in Argos, the mysteries of the Witches' craft at Taurapolis, Necromancy among the graves of Sparta, and incantations in Memphis. Finally in Antioch, drawn by power, you found grace of Christ.

Oh holy Cyprian, you who equally partakes of the mass and the sabbat, bless my efforts to follow you in your path. You who commingled with Angels, devils, and earthly spirits, grant the power to command the spirits as you did, and as Solomon and Manasses did before you.

I thank you lord for the many gifts of nature and grace with which you enriched the spiritual treasure house of your most faithful servant St Cyprian. I thank you, my protector, for the special favors I have received by your powerful intercession.

Oh Cyprian holy thaumaturge: saint and Sorcerer, martyr and magus, bless me. Take my prayers and spells and make them your own. When the lord hears them, he will not ignore them, they will cease to be my words, but yours.

Amen

Take a look at the structure of this prayer. In the first verse we acknowledge the higher power that St Cyprian serves (well, one of them anyway). We follow this immediately by recounting his training. These two verses orient us to the saint and recall his magical heritage. It serves to deepen the connection beyond a mere name, and it serves to focus the prayer on the aspect of his being that we are appealing to.

In the third verse we get into the direct petitioning. We don't just want to talk about how awesome he was, we want him to help us be as awesome as he is. In this case that means consorting with spirits.

In the next verse we thank God for empowering St Cyprian to work on our behalf. Then we thank St Cyprian for past intercession. If you have not received anything yet, thank him anyway. It shows faith he will pull through.

Finally, we appeal to St Cyprian to take our prayers or our spells and make them his because he has this special connection with the Divine. That's the genius about working with saints, you see. God can feel distant. The more powerful and unknowable the deity, the more distant they are. That's why people like intermediary spirits such as saints to take our requests and send them up the chain. We will discuss intermediary spirits in Chapter 10.

Some people don't understand how the saints, described and depicted in ways that highlight their suffering, could possibly provide as much power as Gods and spirits depicted in ways that highlight their power. Their suffering is the key, though. They know what it's like to be human. They know how rough it can be. So, they help and have the insight into how to help best. This is not just the case with Catholic saints; all over the world ancestors and powerful people have been petitioned after their death for intercession.

In the case of St Cyprian we have a saint who stands between heaven and hell, Christian and Pagan, living and dead. Like Hekate, we might describe Cyprian as a liminal figure who is more about the ability to move between worlds than staking a claim to any particular domain, making him (not to mention Justina) a powerful intercessor for those who seek to know the spirits.

SPEAK OF THE DEVIL!

The last few years have seen an embrace of Luciferian and Satanic points of view in a way that has never been open. *The Chilling Adventures of Sabrina* has depicted Satanic Witches in a positive light. In another show, the Devil solves crimes with the LAPD. Scholarly work is being done on Satanism and Black Masses in fin de siècle France. In the United States, there are Satanists going to court to fight for civil rights as well as doing important charitable work. Entire branches of Witchcraft are openly dedicated to Lucifer, Cain, and Lilith. The Devil is surely having his day.

As someone who started practicing Magic in the middle of the Satanic Panic in the late '80s, I am amazed and overjoyed. I am not a Satanist or a Luciferian, but because I'm a Sorcerer operating in the West, he is definitely part of my Witchcraft and my world.

It's important to include this though. Any discussion about consorting with spirits in the West is bound to touch on the classical grimoires. The majority of these books are filled with catalogues of Demons, which are summoned and bound by Christian methods. We will examine these closer in a later chapter, but in this day and age it is worth asking the following question: What would these operations look like if they were summoned by the powers they allegedly align with rather than Heaven? If there is any truth to these rebel Angels serving in a hierarchy of hell headed by Lucifer, then why not summon them through "friendly" powers rather than by the constraint of the enemy?

I follow in the footsteps of Cyprian and work with both Christian and Luciferian powers with no bias against either. To the run-of-the-mill Christian, the division between heaven and hell is as simple as good and evil, but I think if you are reading a book on Sorcery in the 21st century, you probably don't buy that. This doesn't mean the dualist view is not a useful model to play with, but it does mean that we need to do better looking at the roles each plays rather than aligning with one side against another.

In many African traditional religions there is a division of cool and hot spirits, a division similar to the idea of the peaceful and wrathful spirits in Tantra. Those hot spirits are fast to work and powerful at acting, but can be difficult to deal with and are generally not the kinds of spirits you want hanging around the apartment all the time. This is the reason that altars for them are typically kept in shrines and sheds separate from the house. If you have a friend you would want by your side in a barroom brawl but not babysit your kids, then you know exactly what I mean. Everyone has their role to play.

Of course, when it comes to Western Magic with its Angels and Demons, there are some Angels that are so hot they appear as towering columns of fire, and so wrathful that they destroy cities—so perhaps that division is not really sufficient either. Another way to consider it is passion-driven versus wisdom-driven or perhaps egoistic versus ennobled. At the risk of putting the spirits on the couch, perhaps even the Freudian id versus superego is the best way to think of it.

I find this is the best way to think about it: Angels veer toward collectivism and conformity while Demons veer toward individualism and heterodoxy. Sure, there are elements of light and dark and a host of other things, but all these are generalities and maps for our understanding. Always remember that maps are not the same as the terrain.

In practice, all of these divisions have some truth to them yet fall flat from telling the whole picture, so it is tempting to throw out the division entirely, but doing so means throwing out important traditions. So what do we do? We accept that the world is not neat and tidy, and that models are useful until they aren't. Develop discernment.

So back to the Devil. Are you ready for a bit of blasphemy? Try this on for size. If not, then skip it.

Hymn to the Father of the First Flame
The lord said, let there be light
And there was light.
And light rebelled . . .
Without circle or seal
Without foreboding or fear
I call upon the Father of the First Flame
Fallen for freedom's sake
You took your emerald crown from your head
And cast it down into the hearts of man.
By that smaragdine spark I call
Lucifer
Oh morning star
Oh pride untamed
Oh rebel angel
Forever unchained
Opposer, illuminator,
Whose light
Does not fade
Smile kindly upon me
And lend me your aid

If you are seeking knowledge, pray the following after the first prayer:

Oh Lucifer come here to this place that has been bathed
   in light and heat
I am willing to eat of the apple of knowledge of good
   and evil
And accept the cost of gnosis
You who fell for freedom, help free me from ignorance.
As you took pride in your own nature
Strengthen me in my own mind.
Whether through audience, omen, or onieros
Come to me and instruct me in . . .

If it's intercession you are after rather than knowledge, end the
prayer this way instead:

You who refused to bow, help me stand
You who rebelled for pride, help me find dignity
You who detests slavery, and ignorance, and purity
And who compassionately offered Christ the kingdoms
   of the world
Commit again your kindly crime and grant me . . .
To further my own quest for freedom and knowledge

Finally, you should end with the following words that seal the
spell:

Ad lucifer qui laetificat meam.
Veni omnipotens diaboli.
Amen

The last words mean: *To Lucifer who brings me joy. Come omnipotent
devil. Amen.* I realize this is not exactly something your local Sunday School teacher would get behind. Some readers will find this
challenging because they have been raised to think of the Devil
as evil. Others will not like it because Pagans who want nothing
whatsoever to do with either Christ or the Devil have been perse-
cuted as Satanists for a long time. I respect that, and if you don't

Consorting with Spirits

dig this, I encourage you to just ignore it. But for some of you, this might be the kind of spiritual food you need.

COMMON ELEMENTS OF PRAYER

You can probably look at these three prayers and see some common elements. When I was kid, I was taught the acronym "A.C.T.S." for remembering elements of prayer. It stands for Adoration Confession Thanksgiving Supplication.

Adoration can be straightforward praising, or a retelling of great historical deeds, or extolling of virtues and powers. It is useful for orienting your efforts and gaining the attention of the being you are praying to. I mean, who doesn't like compliments right?

Confession is a little trickier for our purposes. Most of us are not worried about being sinners in the conventional sense, but it is still important. Certainly, if you were following the conjurations in a grimoire like *Heptameron* or *The Key of Solomon*, there is significant confession and purification necessary to be ready for the operation. Even if we have no religion we adhere to, or code of conduct we uphold, we all do things that we know lead us away from our goals and ways that we would like to be. Things that take us further from the divine rather than closer. Confession and purification are ways of addressing that.

Thanksgiving is a powerful tool on a number of levels. The first and most basic is that it's polite to thank anyone for their help. If I do a favor for someone and they thank me, I am much more likely to do them a favor in the future. It's not that different with spirits. Gratitude also has a way of increasing overall happiness, satisfaction, and self-worth.

Supplication is simply a request for intercession. Something you would like to achieve that you want some help with. As I mentioned earlier, prayers can stand on their own, or they can be a part of a larger spell and ritual. Candle spells, sympathetic magic, amulets, talismans, and all manner of rituals serve to give your prayers more of a foothold to the material world where we want them to manifest, as well as links to the people and places that we specifically want to affect.

Of course, *all* of this is one-way communication. You are speaking to God or spirit, who does not necessarily answer back. Many people do feel a response to their prayers, but the prayers are not offered with any expectation of Gods or spirits answering directly.

In the next chapter we will open up those lines of communication, starting with local spirits.

CHAPTER 6

Get to Know the Locals

"You are a stumbling moron, and if you did not have strong allies, I am sure the woods would have killed you by now. It is only because of those allies that I am here." Those were the first words that Peggy Clevenger spoke to me, more than 150 years after she died.

Whenever I move somewhere new, I like to research local legends of Witches, Ghosts, Monsters, and assorted occult shenanigans related to where I live. The Pine Barrens of New Jersey are most famous for the Jersey Devil, but there are other spirits who wander the sandy tracks and orange streams that weave between the pines.

Peggy and Bill Clevenger were said to be Witches back in the mid 1800s. When Bill died, he said that if hell was real, he would make the water in the well boil as a sign for Peggy. Whether it did or not is uncertain. What is certain is that Peggy's Witchcraft was well known in the area. People used to say that she would pay for things with gold coins in a sock, and they would turn into seashells in the cash registers after she left a store.

I wanted to get to know the magical landscape of the place that I moved to, so I figured that "The Witch of the Pines" was just the person to help me in my quest, but she was not easy to contact. I started with ceremonies in my temple space at the house. If you can summon a Demon from wherever they are, why not a local Witch?

Well, maybe you can get her that way, but I sure couldn't. At least not in a way I found satisfactory. Sure, I felt a presence, and something would sometimes answer. Magic almost always produces something, but it clearly wasn't Peggy, and it wasn't offering me any information that I didn't already know. I decided to do better.

Rather than going straight to Peggy, I prayed to Hekate, using a method that starts in the simple prayer I shared with you in Chapter 5 and expands from there. Hekate urged me to get off my ass and go hiking to power spots in the Pines. This is where orientation and manifestation come into play.

First, I tried to contact her at one of the blue holes—mysterious circular ponds of blue water that remains cold even in the summer. These are where the Jersey Devil is rumored to emerge from. No luck.

I hiked to the ruins of the well in the Mt. Misery area that her husband allegedly made boil. Nothing. Witches like mountaintops so I attempted to summon her on top of the Forked River Mountain. Nada.

I even tried a conjuration on the beach, but it was no use. I occasionally made contact with spirits, but none of them convinced me that they were Peggy nor any shadow thereof.

I gave up, but Hekate suggested returning to the area that she lived near Mt. Misery (the name sounds like bad horror writing, but I swear it's a real place) and find a three-way crossroads, where I would call upon the Lampads (local night nymphs that can help navigate the spirit terrain of an area). At the next new moon, I found a three-way crossroads in the woods and performed the full ritual, laying out extra offerings for local spirits. After the main part of the rite I called "Mother Clevenger, the Pines Witch" to the western gate of the circle and she came. How did I know it was her? Well, I guess I can't be sure, but spirits who show up at conjurations willy-nilly usually stroke the ego of the summoner and are eager to talk. This spirit's first words to me were, "You are a stumbling moron, and if you did not have strong allies, I am sure the woods would have killed you by now. It is only because of those allies that I am here."

From that point on Peggy would communicate from anywhere in the Pines. She showed me how to use the pygmy pitch pines (mini pine trees whose seed pods only open in forest fires) to cleanse an area and summon Demons. She taught me to use the white crystalline sand as the base of powders for spells. She taught me to summon the Jersey Devil through a blue hole using a wand of black oak, and how to release him using a wand of white oak. In addition, all the Sorcery I did from that point on seemed to take hold better, faster, and stronger than it did before. That's the beauty of having the locals on your side. They get the job done.

ALL SORCERY IS LOCAL

You might wonder what the point of that story was. Well, most Sorcery and Witchcraft are local. There are vast and ancient Gods and Goddesses contactable from anywhere in the world, as well as saints and all manner of spirits, but when it comes to getting stuff done, it's not always who is the most powerful, but who is the most local.

In the famous study of Italian folk Catholicism *Madonnas That Maim*, Michael P. Carroll writes that although the Church teaches that Christ is of primary importance, followed by the Madonna and then the saints, for local townspeople the chain of importance is exactly the opposite. The saint of the town or area is likely to be the fastest at getting things done, and therefore the most important to the locals. They are followed by one of the manifestations of Mary related to your need, and only then by the Trinity, which gets paid lip service while speaking to the beings lower down the chain. This is as magic as magic gets despite it being practiced by good Catholics.

Remember the chapter on how spirits orient themselves? This is where it comes into play. Sometimes even when you talk to a well-known God, spirit, or Demon, your task is handed off to a local spirit. That's why the spirit catalogues in the grimoire list not only the tasks that a Demon is good at, but how many legions he or she commands. Those legions can be local. Local Sorcery is effective. Get it?

This was what Hekate was telling me when I attempted to learn the Sorcery of the Pine Barrens: get with the local spirits—the powerful dead, the local nymphs, the spirits who dwell in the places of power. The land has always played a part in traditional magic, so sometimes this link to the land of origin creates strange issues when it becomes popular in far-away lands.

Many of the Tibetan Sadhanas on my shelf have prayers that refer specifically to protecting and blessing Tibet with no mention of the land that the modern practitioner might be in. Some books on traditional Witchcraft have ingredients that are almost impossible to get here in America, especially when the instructions say to cut them yourself at a particular time. For example, the spirit Apoxias, whom I mentioned in *Protection and Reversal Magick,* first came to me connected to some Hekate workings that I was doing. His request for blackthorn to be included in the bottle prompted many people to inquire about how to get some here in America.[1]

Regardless of what distant land or place of pilgrimage you might hold dear, ultimately you need to recognize the place where you live as a place of magic. If you live in a place famously steeped in occult lore like New Orleans, Glastonbury, or Kathmandu, you have an enormous, if perhaps touristy, body of material to link your Sorcery to. Truthfully, though, the whole world is alive with spirit. Even if you live in the dreariest suburb, surrounded by box stores and blight, you can still investigate the land and integrate it into your practice.

Every place I have ever lived, I have made a map that details the important locations I might need for magic. Once you have this map, mental or on paper, you can begin to establish a relationship with the land and its spirits. It will serve you in ways that you would never expect as long as you serve it faithfully as well.

MAPS AND LEGENDS

I have lived in the city. I have lived in the suburbs. Now I live in a rural town in the mountains of Vermont. I feel very connected to the land here because hiking and kayaking and skiing are the big things to do. There are also not that many people, so it makes hearing the spirits just a little bit easier. You might think that living in a city would be the opposite, but it's not. When I lived in a city, I walked almost everywhere I went, and got to know the city quite well. I found all sorts of magical spots that were teeming with spirit. Parks, monuments, and graveyards all spoke to me with power and clarity. The suburbs presented the bigger problem because it's not quiet like the country—here, unlike the city, you mostly drive everywhere. I had to make special efforts to know the spiritual landscape of town and county, but it was time well spent.

I recommend you start with a little research into the natural geography of your area and look for things of interest. Since the possibilities are as varied as Earth itself, there really is no way for me to tell you everything to look for, but my bet is when you start searching, you will turn up something. Let me give you a few examples.

The Pine Barrens, where I first contacted Peggy Clevenger, was once under water and is now filled with a white "sugar sand" that is primarily quartz. This alone gives the landscape an unusual capacity to manifest astral and etheric patterns. Almost anyone who has spent time in the woods there has some experience with being chased by ghosts or shadows or some kind of paranormal phenomena. This sand makes an excellent spell component as well as making areas like crossed dirt roads extra powerful. Most of the water in the streams there is deep orange because of the overwhelming iron content and runoff from cedars. The iron makes the water a fantastic base for war water or exorcism water.

Strangely, amidst these orange streams there are three circular pools of very deep blue, the blue holes I mentioned earlier. The water in these holes remains cold (around 55 degrees) even in the summer, which has caused several drowning accidents. These holes are thought to have been made by meteorites and the meteoric titanium is what causes the blue hue. The water in these is very useful and the holes themselves seem to be natural gates: areas where the etheric, astral, and material levels condense, and crossover from one to the other becomes easy. Stories of these holes being bottomless and filled with Demons abound in the Barrens.

PEEK BENEATH THE VEIL

After doing some research on the geography of the area, you should investigate with your spirit skills and Sorcery. I used to hike to a blue hole, perform the offering ritual I gave a few chapters back, and then just wait, listen, and look with my spirit skills. What's the point in holding a feast if you don't listen to the guests, right?

You don't need to be in the woods to do this, though. When I was living in Philadelphia, my friends and I used pendulums over maps of the city, followed up by psychic viewing onsite to confirm the existence of a large ley line that ran across the Delaware and west across the city between Walnut and Locust streets. Interestingly, places where these ley lines crossed others (Nexus Points) were at parks: specifically Washington Square, Rittenhouse Square, and Blanche P. Levy Park. One gets the impression that sometimes those city planners knew more than they were letting on. Then again, sometimes spirits of nature take shelter wherever they can as the world of men closes in. Parks seem to inspire both people and spirits to become guardians of them. The first of these parks, Washington Square, not only is the site of hundreds of unmarked graves from the Revolutionary War and the War of 1812, but was known for a time as Congo Square because it was a place where Africans gathered to dance—just like Congo Square in New Orleans, another place of profound power and history.

SPIRITS OF HISTORY

After you dig in to the geography, it is time to crack open the history books. In Philadelphia, there is a cave known as the "Cave of Kelpius" or "The Rosicrucian Cave." Kelpius was a mystic who led a group of self-styled monks known as "The Society of the Woman in the Wilderness" that lived in a system of caves in the Wissahickon woods. Legends abound about Kelpius, including one that claims he possessed the philosophers' stone, which he threw into the Schuylkill River before transmigrating from this life to the next back in 1708. The Ancient Mystical Order of Rosicrucians (AMORC) erected a monolith outside of the cave that he is thought to have lived in. I don't believe that the cave had any innate power to it as a natural spot. It may have even been completely man-made because the inside is fairly square and the door is framed in stone and brick. The power of this spot comes from whatever Kelpius was up to in that cave, and the fact that he and his group made it a focal point for the spirit they were in contact with.

Of course, sometimes you don't need to go anywhere to find spirits from history. In the early 2000s I lived in a house right on Lake Lefferts in Matawan, New Jersey. This lake was the site of the famous 1916 shark attacks during which a great white shark made its way to Long Beach Island, then slowly north into the Raritan Bay, and eventually up creeks into the lakes of Matawan where it killed several children. The story was the basis for the book and movie *Jaws*. I was fascinated that such an odd occurrence happened just ten feet from my dining room, so I spent several nights on the dock making offerings in hopes of contacting the ghosts of the victims and offering some solace. After three nights I made contact with a beautiful Undine who claimed that the shades of the victims were too fragile to receive the offerings, but that she would transmit them for me. Months later, one of these spirits appeared to me in my house to warn me of impending danger from an unstable person I had recently befriended. As it turns out, this warning came in handy and I distanced myself from him before he started lashing out and causing trouble.

Think about this for a moment: I made a simple offering and it was accepted by an intermediary spirit. Some time later, one of those spirits *reached out to me* with useful information. This kind of interchange is exactly what I hope you are able to establish in your life in the place where you live.

THE BONE YARD

Graveyards are the Sorcerer's friend, or at least the home of a few of the Sorcerer's friends. Shades of the dead can be useful in all types of magic. Spirits of murderers and thieves are obviously good for cursing and jinxing. Spirits of soldiers and policemen are likewise good for justice work and also for protection and binding. I seek out the graves and ghosts of recently passed town politicians, councilmen, and businesspeople who are useful for conducting business in town. Obviously the spirits of former magical practitioners are useful allies and dirt from their graves or relics from their lives are sometimes useful for establishing those relationships.

I will be going over Necromancy in a later book, but for now you can certainly work informally with the spirits of particular graves by simply asking them for services and using divination to get the answers. You can also collect graveyard dirt to use in your Sorcery.

Apart from graveyard dirt, dirt from anyplace can be a powerful link, and I often use dirt from all over my environment as parts of spells or as a way to give a spirit a foothold into my world. Dirt from my bank for financial work, dirt from the police station, the town hall, the beach, the mountains, wherever is important.

Graveyard dirt serves as a link to the shade of the person in the grave. To collect it properly, you must pay for it with either a glass of whiskey or a dime. Simply dig a bit from the surface and leave the offering in the hole. This can usually be done during the day with no problem whatsoever. If you do it at night, which is perhaps a better time to communicate with the dead, you should be careful about the laws in your area. Sometimes there is a fine for being in the graveyard at night. Whatever benefit you think you have by doing it at night can easily be nullified by getting arrested.

If you are reading this and going into a graveyard, use discretion and respect. Under no circumstances should you ever dig deeper than a cup full. Don't leave wild, occult-looking ritual implements behind either. Being caught in a graveyard after hours is normally a misdemeanor. Desecrating a grave is much more serious, and also a vile thing to do.

If there is a particular graveyard that you develop an affinity for, have the spirits direct you to the "key grave," a sort of a leader of the boneyard unique to every yard: sometimes it's the oldest grave, sometimes it's the one highest on a hill, sometimes it's a person who held a certain gravitas in life, sometimes it is the grave closest to the gate.

Apart from the individual spirits there, graveyards are excellent spots for meditations on impermanence and working with spirits of death, spirits who are connected to the underworld, not to mention meditating on your own death. My own relationship with Hekate began while I was meditating on impermanence in the charnel ground of Pashupatinath in Nepal, where they burn the dead on the Bagmati River. She appeared in a vision and told me that when I returned to America, I should offer her a supper and she would have things to teach. I did and now two decades later she is still teaching me useful and actionable things.

CHURCHES

Churches, temples, synagogues, and so on are fantastic places to meditate and pray. You do not necessarily have to belong to the congregation or even the religion to make use of them. If you are a person dedicated to truth, which is beyond any specific faith tradition, they are all fair game. If you do a bit of asking around, especially around Catholic and Orthodox churches, you can get the skinny on certain shrines that the community considers powerful. I can tell you that the first time I was ever seriously spiritually attacked, my life was saved at the Shrine of Our Lady of Perpetual Help at a Byzantine Catholic church.

The architecture of many churches is not just inspiring, it is magical! One of the advantages enjoyed by Magicians who work in the Christian tradition is the presence of so many churches. Their spires rise like cellphone towers of spirit, repeating a signal through the land. When you get into old-school folk magic, there is a ton of magic that is based in and around churches. In Sweden, the Årsgång ritual of walking around a church backward on Christmas Eve would empower you to perform Witchcraft, and sometimes reveal the future. Often the rite would trigger an encounter with a Demon or spirit who could initiate you as a Sorcerer.

Some churches are built according to the specifications of spirits. The Swedenborgian Bryn Athyn Cathedral in Pennsylvania is a marvel of spiritual/magical engineering and one of the strangest churches I have ever seen in all my travels. There are no right angles in the whole church, no two hinges or knobs are alike, the roof is made from an unsparkable metal called monel that is almost as heavy as lead, lightning rods run from the roof down into the church, and there is an altar that is a replica of the Ark of the Covenant, which functions like an orgone accumulator. I could go on, but you really would have to see it for yourself to believe it.

WHAT ARE *YOUR* PLACES?

At this point you might wonder why I have been going on about encounters with spirits in places I have lived and traveled. The reason is because everyone's landscape is different, and the best way to show you how to encounter the area that you live is to point out what I do in the areas I live. Please do not feel you need to book trips to the Pine Barrens to gather pygmy pine. The point is to research your area, or areas you would like to travel to, then go and check out those places psychically and magically. Let your research and revelation inform each other, but never confuse one with the other.

If you enflame yourself in prayer and perform regular offerings, the spirits of that place will almost always respond; all you need to do is embrace stillness and listen. You don't need a big ceremony when you can go to the location. Just apply some of the tips and tricks in the spirit skills section on pages 41–54. Once you do, the spirits of an area might give you special instructions that will help you navigate further. For example, while I was trying to gain some kind of knowledge of forests here in Vermont, I would go and touch different trees with very limited response back. Some unseen dryadic spirit whispered in my ear to touch more than one tree at a time. The effect was like touching two points on a circuit, becoming part of that network. As a human I was thinking individually, but the spirits I was trying to learn from didn't work that way.

Prayer and offering are key, but there is one other type of ritual that may help.

COMPASS ROUNDS

Witches and Magicians often work in circles and call spirits to the four compass points that separate them from the ordinary world to keep out unwanted influences. Directional beings don't have to just keep things out though. They can be used to orient you to a spiritual landscape, opening the ways, and attracting spirits to you.

One of my favorite rituals that Hekate taught me is to call upon the four classical winds and the four main rivers of Hades. This arrangement not only calls in the quarters, which we can think of in lateral or horizontal orientation, but calls powers from both above and below. This vertical, or Chthonic Uranian orienting, is key for unlocking the pathways to not only the spirits of nature and the dead, but also the heavens and the underworld.

This connects particularly well to the Hekate prayer I gave earlier, but could be integrated into almost any practice. Give it a try.

> I conjure the divine cup, the graal of gods, which holds
>   all things!
> I conjure the god of aeons, aeon of all!
> Open the pylons of the heavens!
> Open the pylons of the earth!
> Open the gates of the horizon!
> Let me become the nexus of all—the conflux of the
>   winds and rivers
> At the North: **Boreas**
> At the North East: **Acheron**
> At the East: **Eurus**
> At the South East: **Cocytus**
> At the South: **Notos**
> At the South West: **Phlegethon**
> At the West: **Zephyrus**
> At the North West: **Styx**
> Let the winds descend from the heavens
> Let the rivers ascend from the underworld
> Let them meet and meld within me
> Bringing balance of wisdom and power
> Let them blow and flow forth carrying the will of the
>   gods

Send out an offering with an offering gesture and perhaps some incense.

Let the gods be glorified
Let spirits of directions be satisfied
Let the spirits gather and remember
So be it

KINGS OF THE FOUR DIRECTIONS

Another rite you might try is to the kings of the four directions. Depending on tradition there are a lot of sets of directional kings. When I first started practicing Witchcraft, I was introduced to Elemental Kings: Paralda (Air, East), Djinn (Fire, South), Niksa (Water, West), and Ghob (Earth, North). This arrangement of the elements is based largely on the geography around the Mediterranean, and the Holy Land specifically: the arid planes of Jordan to the east, the hot deserts of Egypt and Arabia to the south, the Mediterranean Sea to the west, and the mountains of Turkey and land masses of Europe and central Asia to the north.

You may be tempted to rearrange this elemental arrangement to suit your area, and I have done that too, but keep in mind that it doesn't always work that way. Sometimes it's not about where you are, but where the spirits are from. If you live in Buenos Aires, it would be tempting to put water in the east, fire in the north, mountains in the west, and air in the south because that would reflect where the water, mountains, and sun are in relation to your location, but if the beings you call are oriented elsewhere, it may not work out how you think. How I arrange things is usually determined by what level I think the spirits are oriented to. See how important the idea of orientation can be? If they are oriented locally, I use local elemental correspondences. If they are oriented higher, I use more traditional ones rooted in their origin or tradition.

In Tibet there is another set of four kings related to the directions. It is said that in a time of the Buddha, Dhritarashtra and Virudhaka were Nagas—serpent spirits who were hunted down by birds known as Garudas. These two Nagas sought out the protection of Kashyapa, the Buddha of that age, for refuge. When the Garudas Virupaksha and Vaishravana tried to catch them, they were amazed that they could not harm the two Nagas. The Nagas explained that they had taken refuge in Kashyapa, so the Garudas went to him as well. The four were so moved by Kashyapa's greatness that they promised to reincarnate as protector kings of the directions in the time of the next Buddha—the being we know as Buddha Shakyamuni—in order to support him and his practitioners. Dhritarashtra guards the east, Virudhaka guards the south, Virupaksha guards the west, and Vaishravana—the king of the kings—guards the north. To call to them, face their direction and pray to them in your own words, or use this invocation that I composed:

In the east gate, I call upon the Maharaja Dhritarashtra, great guardian king of the world.
You who are clear white in color, and who command the heavenly Gandarvas, whatever you hear is turned back upon its source so you play upon your vina compassionately. Come forth from the east, guard me, guide me, and open the eastern gate with your pacifying magic.

OM DHRITARASHTAYA SVAHA!
In the south gate, I call upon the Maharaja Virudhaka, the great guardian king of the world.
You who are dark azure in color, and command the fiery kumbhandas, you destroy all that you touch and so you compassionately brandish a sword to keep beings at bay. Come forth from the south, guard me, guide me, and open the southern gate with your fierce magic.

OM VAIRUDHAKAYA SVAHA!

In the west gate, I call upon the Maharaja Virupak-sha, the great guardian king of the world.

You who are clear red in color, and command the watery Nagas, your gaze destroys all that it falls upon and so you compassionately hold your eyes upon your stupa and serpent noose. Come forth from the west, guard me, guide me, and open the western gate with your enchanting magic.

OM VIRUPAKSHAYA SVAHA!

In the north gate, I call upon the Maharaja Vaishra-vana, the great guardian king of the world.

You who are golden in color, and command the yakshas of the earth, your breath destroys all it touches and so you compassionately keep your mouth closed and bestow wealth with your powerful mace. Come forth from the north, guard me, guide me, and open the north-ern gate with your increasing magic.

OM VAISHRAMANAYA SVAHA!

You don't need any kind of special initiation or even to be a Buddhist to invoke the kings of the four directions. Their compassion is not bound by religion, culture, or distance. That said, most of this book focuses on magic and Witchcraft that has its roots in the West and the grimoire tradition, so perhaps we should focus on that.

There are also four kings that are pervasive throughout the grimoires that you should get to know before we move on. They take on great importance in rites of evocation but can be called upon when hoping to make contact with nature spirits, spirits of the dead, or any other type of local or non-local entity.

The kings are sometimes listed as Demons, but most conju-rors I know consider them to have a special liminal status. Like St Cyprian, they are neither of heaven nor of hell, but terrestrial beings who interface with both. This prayer works well either on its own, or you could replace the center portion with the prayer to St Cyprian, the prayer to Lucifer, or a Christian prayer. You have options.

Carry a cup with water, tea, or whiskey, and an incense censor on a chain. Light the incense and swing it three times in each direction as you turn and face them in order. If outside, you can also pour a small bit of liquid as an offering.

Center:
Oh great Metatron, Enoch elevated!
You who stand behind the highest throne and whisper in
    the ear of God.
You are the pinnacle of the temple who distills holy fire
    into oil
Bless this operation and bring me into contact with the
    four regents of the world
That they may open the ways of the terrestrial spirits.

East: Oh you royal spirit Oriens, king of the eastern
    angle. Through divine grace and celestial authority
    given unto our first parents at the time of creation,
    accept my offerings, attend this circle, and open the
    royal roads of the east. Command your legions to
    respond to my requests and do so without delay, delu-
    sion, or disturbance.
West: Oh you royal spirit Paymon, king of the western
    angle. Through divine grace and celestial authority
    given unto our first parents at the time of creation,
    accept my offerings, attend this circle, and open the
    royal roads of the west. Command your legions to
    respond to my requests and do so without delay, delu-
    sion, or disturbance.
North: Oh you royal spirit Egyn, king of the northern
    angle. Through divine grace and celestial authority

given unto our first parents at the time of creation, accept my offerings, attend this circle, and open the royal roads of the north. Command your legions to respond to my requests and do so without delay, delusion, or disturbance.

South: Oh you royal spirit Amaymon, king of the southern angle. Through divine grace and celestial authority given unto our first parents at the time of creation, accept my offerings, attend this circle, and open the royal roads of the south. Command your legions to respond to my requests and do so without delay, delusion, or disturbance.

Return to the east and walk the circle with incense.

Ego me circumcingo virtue horum nominum qiubus hic circulus est consignatus.

I surround myself with the virtue of these names with which the circle has been sealed.

Amen

That last line might make you think that this must be a circle casting or zone rite that sets up a barrier. It can be, but it doesn't have to be. You are, in fact, always surrounded by a circle—it's called the horizon. If you have ever been out to sea, you know what I mean—a water's edge in 360 degrees. All this does on its own is center you, help open channels to the spirits of the area, and make you more visible to them as well.

These particular kings can be a bit distant and cagey. They don't really like to be summoned. That's okay, because you are not summoning them to full appearance. You are asking them to open a door to spirit, to grease the wheels on the divine machinery if you will. You are asking them to open the roads for you. It's resonance you are going for here, not a confrontation.

DON'T NEGLECT THE LOCAL

In Chapter 10 we will talk about Demons and other spirits who appear in books. They are well known enough not only to appear in the most famous books of magic, but to appear on t-shirts, coffee mugs, band logos, and even leggings. They garner a *lot* of attention and debate, not all of it warranted.

Just remember that it's not a game of Pokemon. We are not looking to "catch them all" nor are we always looking for the most powerful spirit. Just like in real life, a few friends in low places can sometimes help you more directly than the powerful and famous.

CHAPTER 7

Fear and Danger

Did you hear about the girl who became possessed by the Babylonian Wind Demon Pazuzu after using a Ouija board? Or about the family who had a pact with King Paimon and all wound up dead? How about the Witch who would make love potions to attract men only to be driven to insanity and death? These kinds of things happen all the time—in movies. Specifically, the *Exorcist* (1973), *Hereditary* (2018), and *The Love Witch* (2016).

Stories of people making deals with spirits that lead to their ultimate demise are timeless. They are to magic what *Reefer Madness* was to marijuana: over the top and unrealistic portrayals of what will happen if you break society's taboo. Like marijuana, the dangers of magic are often overstated by people who know nothing about it other than they were told it's bad. Unfortunately, misinformation can come from the other side as well, and safety can also be overstated. I have seen people push a line of "Nothing bad can happen," or "The spirits love you," which is also not true at all.

Most of us think absolutely nothing about getting behind the wheel of a car and driving to the grocery store even though roughly 38,000 people a year die in accidents on US roadways and an additional 4.4 million people are seriously injured. We do it because the rewards of driving, or getting into a public vehicle, outweigh the risk. We also take precautions when we do it, such as wearing a seatbelt and driving cars with airbags and safety features. If we decided that we wanted to do something particularly dangerous in a car, like race in a derby, we know that our risk increases so we take more precautions as well: a five-point harness, a helmet, a roll cage, and so on.

In short, we take precautions that match the level of risk we face, and we accept that even with precautions there is always the risk of something terrible happening. That's life.

If someone tells you that working with spirits is always going to blow up in your face, I can tell you for sure that person does not actually know much about magic or spirits. I have worked with spirits for thirty years and am doing quite nicely, thank you very much. I know many people who have passed on in their eighties and nineties after living a life consorting with spirits, and there was nothing unusual about their final days. I just spoke last weekend with a Magician who helped me better understand what it means to live with spirits and he is traveling the world at eighty-three years old with a stamina that frankly outpaces my forty-eight-year-old ass. Whenever and however he eventually exits this mortal coil, I would count myself successful to come close.

However, if someone tells you that magic is completely safe, spirits are always friendly, and nothing will ever go wrong, that person either does not know much about magic or they are selling you something based on false pretenses. Again, the rule "just like people" serves us well. Is there such a thing as "all people being harmless, kind, and friendly"? No, there is not. It is the same with spirits.

Taking on the mantle of Witch, Magician, and Sorcerer, and studying the arts of magic should make you more capable in dealing with superstition and fear of the supernatural dark than the average person. Sadly, it often doesn't. I regularly encounter students, some of whom have been "into" magic for years, who hold more unwarranted fear of the occult than their very unmagical neighbors. People seem to have a faith that magic will work well enough to summon spirits, but not well enough to protect you from them. I would say that this is pure church propaganda, but looking at the dwindling numbers of people in pews every Sunday throughout the last fifty years, I don't think that's the case. I think it is horror movies.

The simple fact is that when you are into something, you like to watch movies and shows about that thing. Most movies about the occult are horror movies, so it breeds horror movie thinking. Even the ones that aren't horror movies rarely show magic going as planned. It simply is not a very good plot to have Sabrina use magic and everything goes according to plan. So I will lay the blame on movies. You, however, are not in a movie.

Here is the rule: you already know magic doesn't work like it does in the movies, therefore it's unreasonable to think that the dangers are what they are in the movies.

PROTECTION

Some of you reading this far into the book are probably pulling your hair out over the fact that I have not talked about protecting yourself against spirits yet. I already have you doing exercises to open you up to the spirits, making offerings to attract spirits into your life, and traipsing around graveyards and forests looking for spirit allies. Isn't this dangerous?

Sure. A little.

So you might wonder why this book is so light on shielding and amulets and banishings. Why is this chapter called "Fear and Danger" rather than "Protection Magic"? There are three reasons.

First: I already wrote a book called *Protection and Reversal Magick,* and as I said in the introduction, I am not writing this book with the intention that it be your first foray into magic. If every book has to contain every possible preliminary and protection, then there will never be room for the substance of the book itself. Still,

I look forward to the Amazon reviews complaining that I did not properly instruct people on how to protect themselves.

Second: A short chapter on magical protection can do a disservice to the idea of magical security, which gives the impression that a chapter is all you really need to know for complete and total security. The reality is, whether we are talking magic, or computers, or military installations, there is no such thing as total and foolproof security. Sometimes things will happen that you cannot prevent; all that is left is how to respond. Having confidence that you can respond when shit goes sideways is better than any protective shield or circle. As mentioned, I have already written that book, so I don't want to do it again.

Third, and most important: You can, in fact, have too much security. I call this the *Excalibur* problem. It's not named after the sword, but the 1981 movie of the same name. In that film the characters wear their heaviest armor all the time no matter what they are doing. They fight in it. They joust in it. They eat dinner in it. They screw in it. It's a movie, and it looks cool, so it's fine. In reality, it would be uncomfortable if not impossible. It would be great for jousting when you are on a horse, and might even be okay for fighting (as long as you don't need to move very fast), but for everything else it would actually hamper your experience. Magical security can actually do this too. When 80 percent of your magical practice is "banishing rituals," how open to spirit contact can you be?

There are people who think that they should banish all spirits and unseen forces away from them on a daily basis, so that they essentially live in a bubble allowing contact only with those spirits who they invite deliberately. I tried this approach. Ultimately it's like wearing the armor in *Excalibur* all the time: it cuts you off from the spirits you would be better off meeting and forging relationships with. The same students who come to me hoping to have a vision of a God or Goddess or to hear a spirit give them instructions for a spell are the very same people who banish the heck out of their world every day, which essentially blocks them from the very experience that they hope to have.

When someone is experiencing an active psychic or magical attack, I of course have them banish every day. I have them shield and wear amulets. I have them disengage from most magical practices, even meditation, so that they can protect, heal, and fight back if necessary. You do not want to live your whole life like this.

When I first published an early version of "The Spirit Feast" in *Behutet Magazine* back in the early 2000s, several ceremonial Magicians told me that trafficking with local spirits is too dangerous, and that *real* Magicians only dealt with well-known spirits listed in the grimoires. I was taught this early on, too, but decided it was bunk. Think about it: are you afraid of your neighbors and restrict your interactions only to people listed in a "Who's Who" guide? Of course not! Also, have you ever cracked open a grimoire? It's not like the spirits listed are especially easy-going and chill dudes. On the contrary, the grimoires are filled with warnings about how dangerous they are! Why would I ignore my neighbors in favor of a list of known troublemakers? Now, the idea that all grimoire spirits act like they do in the books is another myth, but we can deal with that in the next few chapters on conjuration.

What I am trying to drive home with this chapter is that managing your fear is just as important as knowing how to protect yourself. I have known students who try extremely hard to have an authentic experience with a spirit who they cannot dismiss as fantasy or an overactive imagination, only to freak out when a spirit appears and speaks. They then shut down whatever they were doing and start exorcising the spirit they just conjured. Don't do that. As my friend and fellow author Sara Mastros once said, "It's rude to play ding-dong-ditch with the spirits."

As a Witch, Magician, or Sorcerer who is trafficking with unseen entities, you should learn to protect yourself. You should have a baseline of protection that covers you in everyday life. You should have operational security that is active during specific workings. You should have response plans in place that are employed only when facing real difficulty and danger.

SPIRITS *ARE* PROTECTION

Rather than worry about any and every spirit you make contact with presenting a danger to you and your loved ones, try to think about how much protection good relationships with the spirits can offer you! Do you know why some countries with little military presence can be invaded while others can't? It's not because of armies; it's because of their pacts with *other* countries that have strong armies.

Spirit allies *are* magical protection. They are actually better spiritual protection than most of your banishing rituals, shields, and amulets. I am referencing so many movies and shows in this chapter, so I will toss one more onto the pile: *The Sopranos*. Do you know why most people are afraid to mess with Tony Soprano? It's not because he is a great fighter, or even that he carries a gun. They are afraid to mess with him because he is in the mob. You don't want to mess with him because even if you kill him, there will be hell to pay.

When I contacted Peggy Clevenger, she told me that I had upset many spirits in my search for her, but that the protective spirits I walked with protected me. If you want that kind of protection, you have to put yourself out there, not live in a bubble. Ancestors, powerful dead, local spirits, Angels, nymphs, fae, and even those grimoire Demons can become allies either through formal pacts or through simple relationships.

This is consorting with spirits.

ROCK ME, ASMODEUS

Back in my twenties my old roommate Matt (who did the art for this book) had moved out a month before our lease was up, so I took advantage of the situation and drew out the complex circle from the *Ars Goetia* on the floor, set out the triangle, and set about evoking spirits using a method as close to the book as I could manage.

The first night I conjured Baal and it went swimmingly well, with a strong response from the spirit and useful answers. The second conjuration of Purson was a bust and nothing discernible came through. I could have kept going with stronger conjurations, but I decided I didn't need to succeed that badly, so I dropped it. The next night's conjuration, focused on Balaam, went as well as the first. The fourth night I decided to conjure Asmodeus. Things did *not* go well.

I can't really say that anything happened that I should have been scared of. There was no horrific appearance or paranormal occurrence. I saw a red light gathering at the center of the triangle and was suddenly gripped by a feeling of danger. I went from feeling calm and cocky to feeling like I was about to be punched in the face. Take the moment that a fist is about to connect with your nose and freeze it. That is what I felt myself trapped in. I immediately thanked Asmodeus for appearing and read the license to depart. To me, that spirit was not to be messed with.

I avoided Asmodeus for years. Twenty years, in fact. I used this conjuration in my teachings as an example that some spirits really are just aggressive. If it's true of people, it's probably true of spirits. I still think that's good advice to keep in mind, but there was more to this than just a bad spirit. That's usually the case with people too.

A few years ago an older and more experienced me read a book called *Sepher ha-Maggid* by Humberto Maggi. This whole book was about Asmodeus and contained fairly simple ways to approach him in a way that is still firm and frank, yet not as aggressive as the methods in the *Ars Goetia*. I decided to give Humberto's methods a go and got quite a different result.

The regal and stern spirit who I conversed with is not what I would call overly friendly, but not needlessly aggressive either. The result I got decades ago was a reaction to the methods I was using, not reflective of the nature of the spirit itself. That's how it worked out for me anyway. Other Magicians report things differently.

As we start to talk about classic operations of conjuration, I want you to keep in mind that assessing risk and managing fear are just as important, if not more important, than protection magic itself.

PROTECTION SPELLS

I still have no intention of filling this book with protection magic. Do some research and gain some competency in your methods of choice. It really doesn't have to be in *this* book for you to use it. That said, here are three short protection spells—prayers, really—that are reflective of the streams of practice we have been focusing on.

A HEKATEAN PHYLACTERY

The following has served me and many students very well.

Aktiophis, shine for me and dispel the darkness of fear.
Whisper to the serpent on my behalf and let him carry
    your will.

Neboutosoaleth, let the moon's light heal me and make
me well.
Strengthen my mind against delusion and deception.
Ereshkigal, hold back the Demons of despair, danger,
and death.
Bestow confidence as I stalk the forbidden and forsaken
Aktiophis, Ereshkigal, Neboutosoaleth,
Sathoth sabaoth sabaoth
Hekate, hear me.
Stand with me and within me
That I may walk forth free from fear and harm.

Angelic Protection

Kneel and face upward, your hands in a position of prayer:

In the name of the most holy IAO I call upon the Arch-
angel Metatron to set
Above me zenith of the cube,
To act as a portal between this space and the
Outermost heavens,
And to protect from all danger and threats that descend
from above.

Stay kneeling and face downward, placing your hands on the
earth or floor.

In the name of the most holy OAI I call upon the Archangel Sandalphon to set beneath me the firm foundation of the cube, to act as a protector from all dangers
that ascend from below.
Stand and face east.
In the name of the most holy AOI I call upon the Archangel Raphael to set in front of me the eastern wall of
the cube, and to protect from all dangers arising from
the east.
Turn and face south.

In the name of the most holy AIO I call upon the Archangel Michael to set on my right hand the southern
wall of the cube and protect me from all dangers
arising from the south.
Turn and face west.
In the name of the most holy IOA I call upon the Archangel Gabriel to set behind me the western wall of the
cube, and to protect me from all dangers arising from
the west.
Turn and face north.
In the name of the most holy OIA I call upon the Archangel Uriel to set on my left, the northern wall of the
cube and protect me from dangers arising from the
north.
Face east again and place your hands in a gesture of
prayer.
A cube within a cube, a world within a world, I place
myself within the adytum, emanated from the pleroma
itself. May the logos sanctify my mind, and the sophia
arise within my heart. Amen.

The Devil's Refuge

This is a spin on Buddhist refuge and Bodhicitta prayers.

I take refuge in the devil, fallen for freedom's sake
I take refuge in the witchcraft, path of wisdom made
power
I take refuge in the damned, cast out, fallen, and forsaken
May all beings have freedom and the causes of freedom
May all beings be free from slavery and the causes of
suffering
May all beings enjoy the freedom that knows no slavery
May all beings live deliciously, free from ignorance and
oppression

CHAPTER 8

Friendly Conjuring

If you went into my garage and pulled down the stairs to the attic, you would see a circle on the floor with seals of the four kings at the quarters. There is an altar in the middle of the circle. On that altar is a wand and a dagger, along with a book of conjurations and a black mirror. A thurible is hanging from the ceiling. It would look more or less like the setup from a classic grimoire that forces spirits to appear by constraining them with divine names and threats. You might think that's what I was doing when I was last in that room, but you would be wrong. I was calling spirits by inviting them rather than demanding that they appear. This is what I like to call *friendly conjuring*.

Unlike simple prayer, in conjuration you expect a spirit to show up in such a way that you can communicate back and forth in that moment. Unlike meeting local spirits in the field, you are not traveling to the place where the spirit dwells, you are calling them to the place where you are performing the conjuration. No operation of magic is more iconic than a Witch or Magician in a circle summoning a spirit to appear.

Just like with people, there are a variety of ways that you can make a meeting happen. Sure, you can flex your muscles and demand that a spirit appear when, where, and how you demand. I would even argue that you should be able to do that when needed. But is that what you want every interaction to be based on? Is that the only trick you want in your toolbox? Is that how you are with people? Jack them up and threaten them to get what you want? I hope not. So why should it be primary mode that you conjure from?

I know that's how the books are written. I don't care. I think history of precedent is important, but I don't live life according to rules that were written when slavery was still legal, so I don't see why my magic should be limited to those books.

The first time I saw a better way of conjuring was when I read *Mastering Witchcraft* by Paul Huson, my first really good book on Witchcraft. In the book, Paul presents an unusual conjuration of the Demon Vassago. Vassago is the third of seventy-two Demons listed in the *Ars Goetia*, one of five books that comprise the Lesser Key of Solomon. This book is easily the most popular collection of spirits people use today, largely because of the complex seals that accompany each Demon. Most people incorrectly refer to the book as "The Goetia," but the word "Goetia" refers to a style of magic, not a book. When referring to the book, you should call it the *"Ars Goetia"* or "Goetia of Solomon" to show the difference. Whatever you do, do not refer to the spirits or Demons in the text as "Goetics" or "Goets."

Huson took the name and seal of Vassago from the *Ars Goetia*, but did not use the conjurations or tools from that book. Long exorcisms invoking the Trinity probably would not have been appropriate for a book on Witchcraft, so he replaced those conjurations with a rather clever system of invitation.

Rather than the Trinity and the saints, he conjures Vassago by "Satandar and Asentacer," the Hebrew and Greek names of the decan of the Zodiac associated with Vassago. Each astrological sign has three decans associated with it, giving a system of thirty-six decans. Some clever person figured out that the seventy-two spirits of the *Ars Goetia* were either linked naturally, or could

Consorting with Spirits

be linked, to the decans: two Demons for each decan. This gives a very tidy alternative power by which you can summon a spirit from the *Goetia of Solomon* without having to boss them around with the rather bossy conjurations from that text.

Apart from the decans that are standing in as higher powers, the name of the spirit gets repeated in three batteries of three throughout the conjuration. Each battery of his name is followed by a request for him to descend from his abode and appear in the mirror or crystal in front of us. There are also praises of powers and great deeds from legend. The goal of such flattery is not to force Vassago down into the triangle, but to entice him down.

Oh, and another difference between Huson's method and the grimoire is that the triangle, typically used to trap the spirit, is on the altar instead of outside the circle. In the *Ars Goetia* you place a triangle empowered by ass-kicking Archangel extraordi-naire Michael on the outside of a protective circle. This places the tricky evil spirit in a trap while you are safe inside a circle surrounded by the names of God and the sephira. In Huson's friend-lier conjuration, the triangle is right there on the altar inside the circle. This changes the dynamic a lot.

The triangle is no longer there to trap an unruly spirit who does not want to be there, but a place for a spirit that has been invited to manifest. The very things that make triangles effective spirit traps also make them powerful platforms for manifesta-tion. They are the most stable and basic structure in our three-dimensional universe and relate to Saturn, a force that establishes the boundaries necessary for things to take shape. The spirit takes advantage of this to gain a foothold into the physical and orient itself to our perception. There is no assumption that we need a lot of protection because from the perspective of Huson's Witch, Demons are a lot less evil and harmful than the church. The Demons will either take the invitation or they won't, so there is no reason to assume things will go sideways. If things do go wrong and a spirit takes advantage of the situation, well, you're a Witch! Deal with it. We will be talking about that in the next chapter. In the meantime, trust me that just like with people, most of the time good intentions, polite demeanor, and respect will get you a long way.

In *The Sorcerer's Secrets*, I presented a Summoning of Bune, another of the seventy-two spirits of the *Ars Goetia*. It was very simple and was meant more as a wealth petition than a full conjuration. I used the decans as powers to call upon Bune, and the Psalm and Thwarting Angel given by Dr. Thomas Rudd as a way of constraining the spirit. I am happy to say that I have gotten many wonderful field reports from readers who tried this summoning and petition. Unfortunately, I also got some hate mail from people who felt that it was dangerous to call upon a Demon without long and wrathful constraints in the name of God! I expect to get even more nastygrams from the "Demons are evil" crowd for what follows, because we are dropping the Angel and the Psalm, and just treating it as a friendly conjuration.

THE CONJURATION OF ASTAROTH

We need a spirit to give as an example of friendly conjuration, so I am choosing Astaroth. As I mentioned earlier, Astaroth is one of the first beings I ever summoned, and I have found her to be friendly and helpful in ways that are barely touched upon in any of the books that she appears in. She is a demonized version of the Goddess Astarte, but because we are using methods rooted in grimoire magic, we will stick to the name Astaroth. That name comes from the Tanakh, where she is called Ashtoreth.

The *Ars Goetia* has Astaroth described as:

> The 29th spirit in order is Named Astaroth, he is a
> Mighty and strong duke, and appeareth in [the] forme
> of an unbeautifull angel, ridding on an Infernall like
> dragon, and carring in his right hand a viper (you must
> not lett him come to neare yu least he doe yu damage by
> his stinking Breath. Therefore ye Exorcist must hold ye
> Magicall Ring nere to his face and yt will defend him he

giveth true answares of things present past and to come and can discover all secreets; he will declare willingly how ye spirits fell, if desired, and ye reason of his own fall. He can make men wounderfull knowing in all Liberall siences; he ruleth 40 Legions of spirits, his seal is as this [shown], wch weare as a Lamen before yu, or else he will not obey you.

A codex found in the Medici Library in Florence, recently translated by Brian Johnson,[1] treats Astaroth, who it refers to as Ascaroth, in a similar fashion, with some added extras:

Ascaroth, a great and strong duke, appears in an angelic form, though his breath is most vile, riding upon an infernal dragon; in his right hand he carries a viper. He gives full, true answers about things present, past, and future; he speaks eagerly of secret things, of consecration; and of their Fall, and how they sinned, and abandoned hope. Having fallen, they marvelously restore to one all of the liberal arts. Every exorcist is to beware of that one Ascaroth, nor shall one permit him to approach oneself while he discharges that intolerable stench from his mouth and advances in immense rebellion; for this reason beware that he not overcome you. Therefore the exorcist shall fearlessly keep a grip on himself and be suffumigated with sandalwood. Having 29 legions.

See how similar these are? Both descriptions of appearance, breath, and so on, are similar. The only differences are in the legions of spirits and how to protect yourself against the demonic halitosis: a ring in the first instance and sandalwood fumigation in the Medici text. You can compare a lot of texts that are nearly all the same. Johann Weyer's *Pseudomonarchia Daemonum* is the same as the Key of Solomon save that it lacks that Astaroth claims not to have fallen from his own accord. The same is repeated again in the *Le Livre des Esperitz*, which seems to be the root text of them all.

The wording is so close that it is nearly unthinkable that the authors of these individual books conjured her[2] themselves. In reality, all these different grimoires are just copies of copies stemming from one conjuration (or perhaps one guy who made up a yarn based loosely on the Testament of Solomon). The point I am trying to make here is that sometimes people treat the descriptions in the books like complete dossiers on the spirits, accurately representing all that they can do and how they will behave toward everyone that conjures them. They are neither.

The *Grimoire Verum* doesn't give a ton of information about Astaroth's nature, but lists her as Ruler of the Americas. This is spot on and really, what else do you need to know? Does this mean that we need to use the seals from the *Grimoire Verum*? Nope. Take a look at the following seals. In my experience, they all work for the same spirit. The first is from the *Grimoire Verum*.

When I decided to include her so prominently in this book, she asked for a variation on the seal in the Goetia that will emphasize her friendly nature. It's just a couple lines that get more slanted than the original, and the bottom cross dropped lower than the pentagram, but sometimes these small changes make a lot of difference when it comes to operative Sorcery.

For our purposes we will be using this seal. If you felt the need to replace it, you easily could.

PURIFICATION

Most grimoires suggest a period of purification before you first contact a spirit. Some treat this merely as a remnant of Old Church thinking and not appropriate for the modern conjuror. I am not too sure about that. What are we purifying ourselves of when we purify? If you think the answer is original sin, then what on earth are you doing reading this book? There are other ways to look at this. We all do certain things that drive us further from the things we say we want for ourselves. The things we hold as right. The things that would lead us toward enlightenment or spirit. We say we want to be healthy, but we eat the bag of cheese doodles and skip exercise. We say we want to be calm, but we rage tweet at someone over something we have no real control over. You get the idea. On a spiritual level there are things we do that drive us further away from the divine, however you conceptualize that.

Another way to conceptualize purification is to think of yourself as a lake that is constantly agitated by storms and turbulence.

You cannot see the bottom of the lake because there is dirt and such always being tossed about in the water. This agitation is just the cost of life and the way we live it. If we can somehow stop that agitation and still the water, the dirt settles and the water is revealed as inherently *pure* and clear. The turbulence is the mental, emotional, energetic, and physical turbulence of daily life. The clarity is the natural state.

If we are seeking to keep company with some subtle beings, it's nice if we make ourselves more subtle. Get it?

So how do we do this? Well, the tried-and-true methods of fasting and abstinence are effective. Every time you think "But I want . . ." and don't give yourself that thing, you are purifying yourself. You are getting stronger and less weak. You are becoming more sublime. Good for you! Of course there are other methods. Confession is effective. It doesn't have to be to a priest. Just confessing to the Gods or even yourself has a way of purifying you. Try some intermittent fasting and some confession for seven days and see how you feel. These are what we would call "outer methods of purification."

Moving from the outer to the inner, if you believe that you have a spirit body, maybe it's important to cleanse the vital channels. I wrote about the nine breath purifications in my book *The Sorcerer's Secrets*. To do this, draw in a deep breath through both nostrils and consider that the air coming in is pure and cleansing.

As you inhale, draw your right arm up at your side so that it is held straight out—this will open up the right channel that handles solar and masculine forces. With the arm still held out at the side, bend your elbow so that your hand is in front of your face, and block your right nostril with your finger. Exhale forcefully through your left nostril, visualizing all impure energies and tendencies leaving the body through the left side.

Do the exact same thing again, but use the left arm to block the left nostril this time, and exhale through the right nostril. Repeat the process twice more for each side, making six breaths in total.

Consorting with Spirits

For the last three breaths simply breathe in and out through both nostrils, cleaning out the central channel. You should again visualize pure air being inhaled and impure air being exhaled. As you exhale, lean forward as far as possible to force the last bit of air out of the channel.

There are other methods of purification, such as the White Star exercise in my book *Sex, Sorcery, and Spirit*, or one of many cleansing baths, but I do not want to spend too much time on it. My experience tells me more than half of you are going to skip the purification step anyway and get right to the conjuring. I admit that I sometimes do that too. The spirits are not going to attack if you are not pure enough. It does, however, help facilitate clearer and deeper contact and communication, so try not to skip it.

Of course if you have a regular practice that you keep up, which includes purification, then you are ahead of the game. This is why I like to stress regular practice in my work.

THE CIRCLE

If you ever look at an image of a conjuration, old or modern, there is probably a circle on the floor. There is some confusion about the role of the circle. If it's a barrier that a spirit cannot cross, then what about everything and everyone outside the circle? No, this is not the same as a circle drawn in the air or a banishing ritual that creates a sphere around you. Those rituals are fine for when you need a wall or barrier, but that is not a floor circle.

The floor circle is not placing a wall of energy that a spirit would bump into if it tried to cross. It is negotiated space, like a demilitarized zone, recognizable by spirits. The power of whatever it is that you have consecrated the circle by will take action against a spirit violating the sacredness of the circle. It's like hallowed ground in *Highlander*, or the Continental Hotel in *John Wick*. There is no bulletproof glass between you and your enemy, but all hell will rain down if you violate the rules of the Continental.

For friendly conjurations I prefer simple circles. One or three concentric rings on the floor will do nicely. No need for names inscribed. In some systems these grease the wheels of the operation, or provide a visible reminder of the powers called to the circle, but in general I prefer a simple circle consecrated in a straightforward way.

When making the physical circle, there are many choices. I have successfully conjured spirits while standing in circles of:

- chalk on the floor.

- tape on the floor.

- leaves in a clearing

- wood that snapped together.

- intricate names painted on floor.

- fancy grimoire designs printed on cloth.

- stones outside.

- white gravel inside.

- marks on a carpet made by dragging my foot.

There are probably a few more things that I am missing, but you get the idea. Please don't get me wrong: I am not telling you to do what you want and that nothing really matters. *Everything matters.* There is a big chasm between the pillars of "This must be done exactly according to these instructions" and "It's really just all about intent." A pox on both of these extremes!

I absolutely think it's worth doing something that shows care and planning. Magicians of the past recorded things for a reason, and to disregard them completely is foolish and disrespectful. To think that we must do things as they have always been done just for the sake of doing it that way is silly. We don't do this with science, with medicine, with art, or even with religion, so we don't need to do it with magic.

Also, people have a tendency to let the perfect be the enemy of the good, and will use the investment of time and treasure they think is necessary as an excuse to never pick up a wand.

For this ritual it is useful, but not absolutely necessary, to place seals of the four kings from the last chapter at the four corners of the circle. They can be painted or drawn on the inside of the circle, or you can simply have them already done on pieces of wood or tile placed at the four corners of the circle as follows:

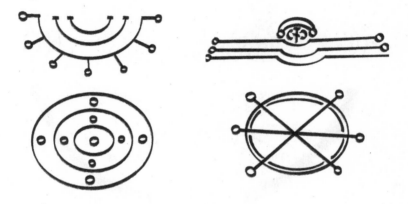

Place an altar at the center of the circle on which you place your conjuring kit. What's in a conjuring kit? I'm glad you asked!

THE CONJURING KIT

Apart from the circle there are some tools that are handy to have on hand. As with the circle, you can invest a lot of time and money into these things. If you start poking around websites and online groups dedicated to evocation and Solomonic magic, you will see some beautiful kits. You can train in woodwork or black-smithing (or both) and make this stuff yourself, which is, I must say, extremely rewarding. You can also spend some cash and get finely crafted items that others make. Like anything else, these range from very high-quality craftsmanship of fine materials, to

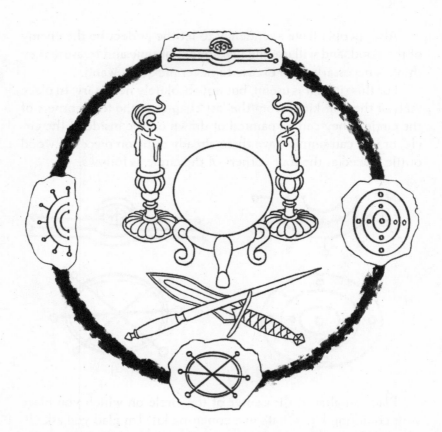

3D-printed or laser-cut boards, to hastily painted or wood-burned stuff from the arts and crafts store.

There are two rules I would like you to remember: First, what you make yourself is not necessarily better. You cannot be gifted in all things, and the power of DIY is overrated when it comes to magic. Second, never let the perfect be the enemy of the good. The main thing is to get to doing the magic. As Krusty the Clown says, "It's not just good. It's good enough!"

To do the rituals on the following pages you will need:

- **A Wand:** Wands are for directing the spirits. Simple enough. Ebony, Hazel, and Almond are all traditional. I have used Oak, Lightning-Struck Pine, Yew, Birch,

Maple, and a metal wand filled with quartz sand and a crystal on it. All worked out okay. Just make sure that it is:

- ° Consistent with the powers you are conjuring in the name of.
- ° Not dedicated to any other specific work (Golden Dawn fire wands and Tibetan Dorjes are not good options).
- ° Consecrated to the powers that you are calling the spirits by. (More on that later.)

- **A Dagger:** This is a friendly conjuring, but you never know what can happen with a new spirit. Just because you are not threatening the spirit with it does not mean it's not a good idea to have it on hand. Choose a nice dagger with an iron or steel blade. I have used boot knives, fantasy daggers, hand-forged blades made by Magicians, and so on. The same three rules apply to daggers as they do wands. If you are conjuring in the name of YHVH, your Wiccan Athame is not a good choice. If you are conjuring in the name of your Witch Gods, then it is probably a great choice. Do not use a Phurba as a dagger.

- **A Thurible:** This is also known as an incense burner. You can use stick incense if you like, but a thurible on a chain is a nice accoutrement to have in the circle. With a thurible and charcoal you can blend your own incense for each spirit, or an incense that aids in your own psychic perception. Being able to ritually swing it on a chain is a nice way to smoke the incense on certain parts of the circle. This can be done as an offering to the spirit, or as a protection when needed, as the Medici text indicates. Honestly, incense on a thurible can do it all. You can create a circle, create a hospitable place to manifest, direct a spirit, and defend against a spirit, *all* with suffumigation.

- **A Scrying Device:** This is something you want the spirit to appear in. You don't actually *need* one of these. In a friendly conjuration, the spirit will often appear at the edge of the circle or communicate in ways that are less visual. Part of being friendly is being a little less high maintenance in your demands about whereexactly the spirit shows itself. However, another part of being friendly is giving options to your guests. Having a scrying device, or even more than one, can be a boon to a spirit that is struggling to make themselves known to you.

If you are already practiced at scrying in a black mirror, there is no reason to switch to a crystal and vice versa. I use both. I love the way that my borderless concave black mirror, literally a glass clockface with the convex side painted flat black, creates the appearance of a hole in space. When I use the dimensional gazing technique that I mentioned in Chapter 3, this mirror responds vibrantly. I also love a small quartz crystal I used in a ritual with Ivo Dominguez. I let my eyes start tracing the many occlusions in the crystal inward and soon things begin to appear not so much *in*, but *through* the ball.

CONSECRATION OF TOOLS

How do you consecrate the previously mentioned tools? I suggest the KISS formula: Keep It Simple, Stupid.

Okay, you're not stupid, but we all get kind of stupid sometimes with overcomplexity. This is especially true in books like this. I have pages to fill, after all, and I hope to provide something that captures your attention. Ironically the longer and more impressive the rituals are, the more the text might get valued, yet the less people will actually do the stuff. That's not what I am about, so keep it simple.

Method 1: Asperse it in Holy Water and say "By the power of X, I purify this (wand/dagger/thurible) that it may serve as an implement of the art magical. In the name of X, I consecrate thee. Amen."

Method 2: Anoint it with appropriate oil and say, "By the power of X, I annoint this (wand/dagger/thurible) that it may serve as an implement of the art magical. In the name of X, I consecrate thee. Amen."

Method 3: Light some incense and set out a bowl of salt water. Pass through the incense and say, "By the power of X, this (wand/dagger/thurible) is purified by all powers of Air and Fire that it may serve as an implement of the art magical. In the name of X, I consecrate thee. Amen." Then sprinkle some salt water over it and say, "By the power of X, this (wand/dagger/thurible) is purified by all powers of Water and Earth that it may serve as an implement of the art magical. In the name of X, I consecrate thee. Amen."

Are there more advanced methods? Yes. Feel free to use them. You can also combine these all together or just use water and oil or use the elements and oil. Basically you just need to make the tool sacred. You purify it and mark it as special, thus making it more relevant and visible to the spirits you work with. You also mark it as sacred to the power that you are calling the spirits by.

You can use this method for pens, inks, mirrors, skulls, and anything else you please. The only rule is that once it is consecrated, it should be kept with your magical tools, not just thrown back in a drawer. So don't go blessing everything you own, or you are gonna have sacred storage problems. Consecrated t-shirts might seem like a good idea, until you realize you are committed to storing it somewhere sacred and you can't give it to Goodwill when you get tired of it.

THE SEALS OF THE SPIRIT

There is one last tool to talk about. The one that gets the most attention. Probably more attention than it should. I am speaking about the seal of the spirits.

Spirit seals look cool. That sounds trite, but actually the cool-factor winds up affecting the way people practice magic. For instance, Luciferians in America and Europe seem to love this seal from the *Grimoire Verum* and have adopted it as *the* seal of Lucifer. The thing is that in the book, it's the seal of Lucifer *in Asia*. In Europe you are supposed to use a different, far less bad-ass looking seal. Now, it may very well be that the popularity of the seal should be read as the Morningstar giving his approval to this seal. Even if that is not the case, things evolve and change over time, so there is nothing wrong with that seal gaining precedence. I mention this because we should be aware of how the cool-factor affects the spread of these traditions. Art matters.

The seals of the seventy-two spirits of the *Ars Goetia* are pretty bad ass. You can purchase them as pendants online in all sorts of materials, and most of these would work nicely for ritual. You can also purchase coffee mugs, t-shirts, bracelets, fleece blankets, and leggings. Most of these are *not* useful for ritual. I dare say it might even be a bit problematic to have the seal that you are using to attract the Demon on your cup of morning joe.

Because seals are part of the ritual in the Lesser Key of Solomon, as well as other grimoires like the *Verum*, the *Red Dragon*, and so on, some people believe that you need a seal to summon a spirit. *You don't.* Like most ingredients, it's nice to have, it can help, but it's not a make-or-break component. There are plenty of grimoires that contain spirit catalogues with no seals, including the ones that laid the foundation for the *Ars Goetia*. The name will more than suffice. In Tantra they say that the mantra of a Yidam or Dakini is inseparable from the being itself. I believe the same about the seal and the name of a spirit. If you have a name, that is the most important element. That said, seals are beneficial.

START THE CEREMONY

We have purified ourselves (or not), gathered our tools, and set our circle on the floor. It's time for the ceremony.

Begin by establishing the circle. Just a reminder: a circle is more than protection—it's dedicated space for something to happen. Also, even though this is done with the intention of inviting rather than commanding a spirit, we cannot guarantee the spirit, or the legions under that spirit's control, will behave how we want them to, so some protection is in order. I go to the edge of the circle and walk clockwise around while swinging the burning incense and repeating the following:

Gyrum carpo! (I seize the circle)
Consecrro et benedicto istum circulum (I consecrate and
    bless this circle)
Per nomina dei IAO (In the name of IAO)
Ut sit mihi et omnibus scutum et protectio (That it be for
    me and all an invincible shield)
Dei fortissimi IAO invincibilie contra omnes malignos
    spiritus gerurmque potestates (and a fortress against
    evil spirits and powers)
In nomine dei IAO. Amen. (In the name of IAO. Amen)

This is loosely based upon a conjuration in the seventh book of Moses. I like IAO as a God name to conjure by. It is more Gnostic and less Bible-based than YHVH, but still in that stream of power that spirits of the grimoire traditions are used to responding to. I will demonstrate how to work Pagan or Luciferian variants shortly, but when you change the powers that you conjure and consecrate by, it does more than just change a word. It changes the nature of the whole operation!

Once we return to the east, we can move back to the center of the circle and address the kings of the four directions. These four kings are yet another power that the spirit is conjured by, and they greatly aid in helping the spirit appear. Think of them as road openers: they are not only there for protection and command, but for helping communications.

Face east and wave your wand three times: once to the left, once to the right, and once to the center. Keep your wand pointed at the center and say:

O Uriens, king most shining, who reigns in the east, whose kingdom has had commencement at the begin-ning of the world and which will endure until the end of the ages. By the power of IAO I humbly yet frankly demand that you open the gates of the east. Let my con-jurations echo loudly in the east and your seal serve as a key to your kingdom. Let all spirits who are subject unto your command appear promptly and be subject unto me when called.

Face south and repeat the waving. Point and say:

O Maymon, king most noble, who reigns in the south, whose kingdom has had commencement at the begin-ning of the world and which will endure until the end of the ages. By the power of IAO I humbly yet frankly demand that you open the gates of the south. Let my conjurations echo loudly in the south and your seal serve as a key to your kingdom. Let all spirits who are subject unto your command appear promptly and be subject unto me when called.

Face west and repeat the waving. Point and say:

O Paymon, king most glorious, who reigns in the west, whose kingdom has had commencement at the beginning of the world and which will endure until the end of the ages. By the power of IAO I humbly yet frankly demand that you open the gates of the west. Let my conjurations echo loudly in the west and your seal serve as a key to your kingdom. Let all spirits who are subject unto your command appear promptly and be subject unto me when called.

Face north and repeat the waving. Point and say:

O Egyn king most strong, who reigns in the north, whose kingdom has had commencement at the beginning of the world and which will endure until the end of the ages. By the power of IAO I humbly yet frankly demand that you open the gates of the north. Let my conjurations echo loudly in the north and your seal serve as a key to your kingdom. Let all spirits who are subject unto your command appear promptly and be subject unto me when called.

You don't need to feel the presence of the kings or have any response from them at all. It is the fact that their names have been dropped that does the trick. It does help to have the seals in the four directions, but you don't even strictly need that. Their names carry weight.

THE CONJURATION OF ASTAROTH

Place the seal of Astaroth around your neck or hold it up in front of you. Some people feel like they need to stare at the seal, but that is not really what it is there for. It is a sign to the spirit, not something for you. Circumambulate the inside of the circle once in silence and then face east, the direction Astaroth usually comes in from. If for some reason you sense that the spirit comes from another direction, you can orient there instead. There are traditional directions associated with many spirits, but honestly, I usually wing it and feel it out. I once asked a spirit why he came from the north when the book says he comes from the south, and he pointed out that the book was written more than 200 years ago and things change.

Anyway, when you return to the east, say the following:

By Yasyasyah and Epimah
I conjure thee
O thou great and holy
Asteroth! Asteroth! Asteroth!
Vouchsafe to descend from thy abode,
bringing thy influence and presence into this glass (or
    crystal, or bowl, or the edge of the circle, or simply
    into this chamber . . .)
that we may behold thy glory and enjoy thy society
    and aid!

Again circumambulate the circle clockwise at this point, returning to the east as before to continue:

By Yasyasyah and Epimah
I conjure thee
O thou great and holy
Asteroth! Asteroth! Asteroth!
Great Duke of Hell
Who knows the secrets of Babylon
And who rides upon the great dragon of magic
do thou descend and be present I pray thee . . .

Circumambulate yet once more and finish the invocation:

By Yasyasyah and Epimah
I conjure thee thrice three times,

Asteroth! Asteroth! Asteroth!
to descend and appear to us within this glass (or, ya
know, whatever . . .)
speaking secrets of truth and understanding.

Feel free to change all the "thee" and "thou" to modern "you" and "your" if you like. I like the language the way it is; it marks it as something sacred and different than ordinary speech.

Spend some time in front of the crystal or mirror and see if she appears. If you feel a presence but cannot see her, repeat the preceding section with more force. Keep in mind this script is a light *request* to appear. The power of the decans is such that it will get the spirit's attention and press the spirit lightly, but will not force an unwilling spirit.

If all goes swimmingly, you can use your spirit skills to check the crystal or mirror for any appearance. Look to the edge of the circle and the incense smoke. You don't have to delve deeply at first; let the spirit reach out to you. Just be silent and don't do anything. Wait for a response.

Patience is key. Spirit evocation of any kind depends on alternating between sending and receiving. Some people get so into the conjurations that they destroy their ability to sit and perceive. Others get so into the idea of receiving that they stay open long enough to interpret anything from a stiff breeze to a hiccup as a communication. Balance these.

After a reasonable amount of time, repeat the conjuration (not the circle opening). As you speak the words, listen for how you hear your own words and understand them. You don't do it in the ears; you do it in the mind. Feel how that happens and reach back out from the mind to see if there is anything else coming through. It works the same with sight. Your eyes don't construct the things you see; your brain does. Spend some moments feeling for how that happens, then reach out again and see if you can sense a bit *more*.

If the second conjuration doesn't work, you can try a third time, but that's it. More than that is rude, and we don't want to do that in a friendly conjuration. The spirit may appear later in your dreams or give omens after the operation.

If Astaroth appears or communicates in some way, this is where the conversation starts. Ask questions and listen for answers. Ask if there is anything different that you can do next time to make contact easier, faster, or clearer. Roll with whatever happens when it's happening. If you suspect you may be fantasizing, that is something to examine after the working. For now, just engage the experience.

When you are ready, give the license to depart:

> O great and holy Astaroth
> we license thee depart into thy proper place
> and be there peace between us evermore
> By Yasyasyah and Epimah
> I hereby close all gates, and dismiss this circle.
> Amen

CONJURE OTHER DEMONS WITH THIS METHOD

Obviously you can use this technique to conjure any of the spirits in the *Ars Goetia*, you just need to switch the decans to fit the spirit. This list provides the Hebrew and Egyptian names from Aleister Crowley's 777 for each spirit of the *Goetia of Solomon*. There are many other decan names you can choose from and I recommend the book *36 Faces* by Austin Coppock for the best treatment of the decans anywhere. I have tried different sets of names, but they do not seem to add any serious effect to the operation, so I keep to the list that worked for me when I started summoning spirits in this way.

This is a much lighter operation than doing the grimoire by the book, but the result is *exactly the level of contact that I find most useful*. Methods that rely on stronger methods will be surer to conjure the Demon to appear whether it wants to or not, and will give you more direct control over the spirit when it appears, but in my life I

Consorting with Spirits

have never wanted to work with a spirit, or a person, that needed a massive amount of handling. It is not my style.

If you want to summon a different spirit, choose its name from the following list, and just replace Yasyasyah and Epimah with the appropriate decans. You can check the *Ars Goetia* for the corresponding seal. That just leaves a few lines that need to be changed to fit the spirit.

In this conjuration we call Astaroth "Great Duke of Hell Who knows the secrets of Babylon and who rides upon the great dragon of magic." These lines were chosen by me based upon the history of Astaroth and descriptions in the grimoires. Paul Huson made reference to Vassago knowing the secrets of Elanel, riding on the wings of the wind, and his superlunary motion. If I was conjuring Zepar, I might praise his ability to make people fall in love with one another or his red armor and martial appearance. The tiniest bit of research and poetic license will give you a few lines that are particular to the spirit you wish to call.

Maybe one day I will print a chapbook with lines for every spirit, but it's worth doing a bit of research and putting a bit of yourself into the conjuration. Effort is rewarded.

Demon Name	Hebrew Decan	Egyptian Decan
Bael	רזז Zazer	Assicean
Agares	ימההב Behahemi	Lencher
Vassago	רדנטס Satonder	Asentacer
Gamigina	ידמדכ Kadamidi	Asicath
Marbas	יארחנמ Minacharai	Virvaso
Valefor	זונגסכי Yakasaganotz	Aharph
Amon	שרגס Sagarash	Thesogar
Barbatos	ינדהש Shehadani	Verasua
Paimon	וןתיב Bethon	Tepistosoa
Buer	שוארתמ Mathravash	Sothis

Demon Name	Hebrew Decan	Egyptian Decan
Gusion	צדהר Rahadetz	Syth
Sitri	ריכנילא Alinkir	Thuismis
Beleth	רהנסול Losanahar	Aphruimis
Leraikha	יעחז Zachi	Sitlacer
Eligos	רביהס Sahiber	Phuonidie
Zepar	הרואננא Ananaurah	Thumis
Botis	הידיאר Rayadyah	Thoptius
Bathin	רפשמ Mishpar	Aphut
Sallos	ינסרט Tarasni	Serucuth
Purson	צנרהס Saharnatz	Aterechinis
Marax	רדחש Shachdar	Arepien
Ipos	צומכ Kamotz	Sentacer
Aim	רהודנג Nundohar	Tepiseuth
Naberius	לאידורתו Uthrodiel	Senciner
Glasya-Labolas	תארשמ Mishrath	Eregbuo
Bime	וירהו Vehrin	Sagen
Ronove	אהובא Aboha	Chenen
Berith	וונסמ Misnim	Themeso
Asteroth	היסיסי Yasyasyah	Epima
Forneus	לאידורבידגסי Yasgedibarodiel	Homoth
Foras	מפפס Saspam	Oroasoer
Asmoday	וורדבא Abdaron	Astiro
Gaap	לאידורג Gerodiel	Tepisatras
Furfur	ימלהב Bihelami	Archatapias
Marchosias	וורוא Avron	Thopibui
Stolas	וירטס Satrip	Atembui

Demon Name	Hebrew Decan	Egyptian Decan
Phenex	רזז Zazer	Assicean
Halphas	ימההב Behahemi	Lencher
Malphas	רדנטס Satonder	Asentacer
Raum	ידמדכ Kadamidi	Asicath
Focalor	יארחנמ Minacharai	Virvaso
Vepar	ווגנסכי Yakasaganotz	Aharph
Sabnock	שרגס Sagarash	Thesogar
Shax	ינדהש Shehadani	Verasua
Vine	וותיב Bethon	Tepistosoa
Bifrons	שוארתמ Mathravash	Sothis
Uvall	עדהר Rahadetz	Syth
Haagenti	ריכנילא Alinkir	Thuismis
Crocell	רהנסול Losanahar	Aphruimis
Furcas	יעחז Zachi	Sitlacer
Balam	רביהס Sahiber	Phuonidie
Alloces	הרואננא Ananaurah	Thumis
Camio	היד יאר Rayadyah	Thoptius
Murmur	רפשמ Mishpar	Aphut
Orobas	ינסרט Tarasni	Serucuth
Gamori	ונרהס Saharnatz	Aterechinis
Oso	רדחש Shachdar	Arepien
Amy	וומכ Kamotz	Sentacer
Oriax	רהודננ Nundohar	Tepiseuth
Napula	לאידורתו Uthrodiel	Senciner
Zagan	תארשמ Mishrath	Eregbuo
Volac	וירהו Vehrin	Sagen

Demon Name	Hebrew Decan	Egyptian Decan
Andras	אהובא Aboha	Chenen
Haures	ונסמ Misnim	Themeso
Andrealphas	היסיסי Yasyasyah	Epima
Kimaris	לאידורבידגסי Yasgedibarodiel	Homoth
Amdusias	ספפס Saspam	Oroasoer
Belial	וורדבא Abdaron	Astiro
Decarabia	לאידורג Gerodiel	Tepisatras
Seere	ימלהב Bihelami	Archatapias
Dantalion	וורוא Avron	Thopibui
Andromalius	ףירטס Satrip	Atembui

CONJURE SPIRITS UNDER DIFFERENT POWERS

Now we come to a very hot topic in the world of magic: can we conjure these spirits without invoking the God of Abraham?

The answer is yes, but it's not quite as simple as just switching out one God for another. It changes the nature of the conjuration. Think about it: the names and seals of these Demons came about through Magicians and exorcists conjuring them using mostly Christian, and sometimes Jewish or Muslim, formulas. Someone somewhere grabbed these seals from the spirits and got them to respond to them. In all likelihood those operations were done with conjurations invoking Adonai, YHVH, and so on. I use IAO as a way of linking back to the era of the *Greek Magical Papyri* when Magicians pulled whatever worked from the various cultures that were colliding in the 2nd-century Mediterranean—a period not unlike now in many respects. But IAO is still linked to the God of Abraham, if a bit more loosely than other names.

So what happens if you call upon Astaroth under the power of Hekate? Does everything stay the same? Does the spirit respond the same? Is the seal even a meaningful thing in that context or should new seals be developed? Do you use the four kings or switch to something like the four winds? I have done this with mixed results. Some spirits seem to respond the same, others are more eager, and still others are resistant. Just like people, the details of relationships can be complicated. Cookie-cutter approaches to complex issues like this should be avoided.

What about Lucifer or Satan as a power behind the evocation? Satan is a Christian spirit, just on the other side of the fence. If we engage the idea that these spirits are seventy-two Demons, then what happens if we conjure them under the powers of hell (the powers they serve), rather than heaven (the powers they rebel against)?

It goes a little like this:

Gyrum carpo! (I take/seize the circle!)
Ego (name) consecro et benedico istum circulum (I, (name) consecrate and bless this circle)
Per nomina dei diaboli (in the name of the devil)
Ut sit mihi et omnibus scutum at (that it may be to me and all a shield and)
Protectie fortissimi lucifer invicibile (protection in the name of the most powerful invincible Lucifer)
Contra omnes malignos spiritus (against all malignant spirits)
Eorumque potestates in nomine Satanam inferi (and powers in the name of Satan and all infernal powers)

Invoke the four kings as you do in the previous conjuration.

In the name of the son of morning,
The dragon of lamentation,

And the angel of exile I move you with the fire of the first flame:
Asteroth! Asteroth! Asteroth!

By Yasyasyah and Epimah I conjure thee o thou great
  and unholy
Asteroth! Asteroth! Asteroth!
Vouch safe to ascend from thy abode, in the name of
  Lucifer your emperor bringing thy influence and presence into this glass, that we may behold thy glory and
  enjoy thy society and aid!

Again circumambulate the circle clockwise at this point,
returning to the east as before to continue:

By Yasyasyah and Epimah I conjure thee o thou great
  and unholy
Asteroth! Asteroth! Asteroth!
Great duke of hell who knows the secrets of Babylon and
  who rides upon the great dragon of magic do thou
  descend and be present I pray thee . . .

Circumambulate yet once more and finish the invocation:

By Yasyasyah and Epimah
And by the emperor Lucifer I conjure thee thrice three
  times,
Asteroth! Asteroth! Asteroth!
To ascend and appear to us within this glass speaking
  secrets of truth and understanding

A few notes: we are invoking Astaroth under the power of
Lucifer the Emperor of Hell. We use some titles that tie into the
Lucifer legends for this. We use the term "unholy," not to denote
evil, but to say that it is not separated from the worldly things
in the way that something consecrated under the Christian God
is. There is an embrace rather than rejection of worldly powers.
Beyond that, the conjuration is basically the same.

If you find this previous section repugnant, don't use it. Suffice
to say many people feel the same about the Christian God. I am
basically an animist, so I see them all simply as powers and spirits: heaven representing a valid spiritual path that is more about

collectivism and rejection of worldly temptations, and hell representing a valid spiritual path that is more about individuality and engaging the poisons of the world alchemically. I could go on about it, but really that's a topic for a whole other book.

It's time now to talk about conjurations that are less about inviting spirits and more about compelling them.

CHAPTER 9

Compelling Conjurations

I have seen people refer to traditional grimoire evocation as the opposite of exorcism. On the surface this makes sense. In evocation you are drawing a spirit to you; in exorcism you are pushing the spirit away from you or another person, place, or thing. Thinking of evocation and exorcism this way makes sense from that perspective, but it's misleading. In truth, evocation and exorcism are nearly the same thing.

The word "exorcism" comes from the Greek word "Horkizo," (to bind by oath). It is this underlying action, binding a spirit by oath that compels a spirit to do what you command, that is at work in both exorcism and evocation. Whether you are commanding the spirit to leave a possessed person or inhabit a triangle with a crystal in it is almost beside the point. You are still compelling by oath.

If you want to look at the threads that tie into the Western grimoire tradition, Catholic exorcisms feed into it just as much—if not more than—*Greek Magical Papyri* and other occult influences. Many manuscripts refer to the would-be summoner in their instructions as "the exorcist." This is both because the summoner is binding the spirits to appear by oath and because he often would hold apostolic consecration. Even if he did not hold the major orders of deacon, priest, or bishop, he still might have received minor orders such as acolyte, lector, or exorcist.

In the case of a possessed person or haunting, it's easy to see why an exorcist would be handy to kick out an entity that is already there, but why on earth would anyone want to deliberately and aggressively seek out Demons and then bind them into service? If we can ask spirits for their aid, or make mutually beneficial pacts with them, why would we want to start off like Karen demanding to see the manager? Why would we be bossy?

WHY BE BOSSY?

There are a lot of reasons to be bossy. A few of them are even *good* reasons, but before we get to those, let's take on the mindset of a Renaissance-era Christian Magician.

If you believed that the Demons in the books are legit "fallen" and "damned" spirits that are up to no good, then why wouldn't you want to bind them? I mean, if you have a bunch of unruly troublemakers loafing about causing teeth-grinding and wet dreams, wouldn't it be better to give them a job to keep them busy? If you can manage to get laid and paid in the process, then all the better, right? According to legend, these are the Demons that Solomon forced to build the first temple. If it's good enough for that wiseguy, it's good enough for John Q. Magus, right?

It should be clear by now that I don't buy into the fallen Angel/agents of evil bit, but if you did, or if you do, think along those lines: it makes a lot of sense. Even if we don't believe these spirits to be inherently evil for evil's sake, they can still be dangerous. Dividing the spirits along some form of dichotomy is done all over the world. Tibet has peaceful and wrathful spirits. Vodou has nations of lwa that are considered hot and others that are cool. Irish Fairies get divided into the Seelie Court (kind and helpful) and the Unseelie Court (antagonistic). Greeks had their

Olympian and Chthonic spirits. Christians have their Angels and Demons.

Let's make this simple. Think about day and night. The night isn't evil, but it's recognized as more dangerous. It's not as easy to see. Wilder things tend to happen. If someone does have evil intent, it's often a lot easier to sneak up on someone or get away unseen at night. If you can understand this, you can understand why a dualistic division of spirits is simultaneously useful, yet nowhere near universally true.

So why be bossy? Because it gives a bit more control over those wild and dangerous types. If you go in and flash your badge and gun, throw the informant up against a wall, and threaten punishment if they don't do *exactly* what you tell them to do, that is a way of establishing and maintaining control. You are doing it with a dagger and a seal.

Of course, doing this also has a downside. No one likes to be treated this way, so although they may do the bare minimum needed to fulfill a pact, they are unlikely to care about the outcome for you. They fulfill the agreement to the word, but not the intent. This can sometimes lead to *the ham sandwich problem*. As in "Genii, make me a ham sandwich!" Zap! You're now a tasty ham sandwich!

Most of the time a spirit will respond exactly as you demand that they do. You are compelling them, after all. Sometimes you will get a negative result or pushback, in which case you kind of *have* to keep going with stronger conjurations. That's the thing about compelling someone to do something: once you start, you are locked into that approach. It takes a massive amount of work to be buddies with someone that you previously imprisoned and compelled.

So, should you always start off with a friendly conjuration? Not necessarily. Some spirits will only respect you once you have compelled them. Some spirits will be very eager to be friendly but take advantage of you without the threat of compelling. It's complicated. Just like people, there is no such thing as all spirits acting a particular way.

So what do you do? If different spirits can act differently to different approaches from different people, how are we to know which one is right?

You can't. So don't try.

Here's my rule: don't morph into the person that you think will best suit them. Instead, think about who *you* are, and how *you* want your interactions to go. It's probably similar to how you would act with people. If you are a person who needs to know that they have leverage on people before they strike a bargain, then chances are you will not feel safe or comfortable with spirits until they are compelled, and you are certain that you are the one in charge. You know what? That is okay. "Know thyself" is the central rule.

If you are more like me, and would prefer relationships based on friendly beginnings, then you will rely more on friendly conjurations than the compelling methods that demand appearances in a particular way. If a particular spirit doesn't want to appear, or doesn't want to help, just pack it in. There are plenty of other spirits who will.

You might be thinking that maybe you don't want to mess with compelling spirits at all, and that if you just stick to the friendly conjuration, you will be better off.

Not so fast. . . .

You certainly can stick to friendlier and more egalitarian methods, but that doesn't mean every spirit you reach out to will respond in kind. Just like people, some spirits will take advantage of soft approaches. Some spirits will cause trouble just to see what you are made of, then settle down when you establish that you can't be pushed around.

Now, in the case of people, if you invite someone over and they start trashing your house, you can call the police. If it's a spirit that you have invited over and they start rampaging through your life, who you gonna call? I know . . . I know . . . Ghostbusters. Seriously though, you need to be able to have a moderate familiarity with exorcism and binding spirits. Even if you hope to never use it, you still need to have it. Like Teddy says, "Speak softly and carry a big stick." Or maybe a wand or sword in this case.

CONTROLLED APPEARANCE

There is another reason that Magicians rely upon compelling methods, and it has to do with the orientation of the spirit. Remember in Chapter 1 where I laid out astral, mental, and causal levels to which consciousness can be oriented? I also mentioned that many Gods, Angels, and Demons are oriented to some fairly subtle levels not close to the physical. When you pray or contact them, they often come very subtly, and rarely can you point to a specific place that they are coming from.

This is different when you use strong evocations or exorcisms. Compelling methods don't just force a spirit to appear, they determine the way in which the spirit appears. This is a key concept and one of the biggest attractions of conjuring. It gives several advantages.

The biggest benefit is that compelling conjurations are designed to make a spirit appear to the naked eye. Not to finely honed spirit senses, but the ordinary naked eye. That does not mean you would get it on camera, but it does mean that you would be able to see it in the way you see a mirage or hallucination. You don't have to try to see; when you pull this off, the spirit is just there. In a really strong appearance, you look away from the spirit, then look back and it's still there.

This, however, is not necessarily a comfortable position for the spirit to be in, and there are many records of evocations where the spirit is anxious for the conjuration to end. It does, however, have the benefit of making for clearer communication—much more akin to a conversation with a person.

This level of manifestation does not require much in the way of psychic development or spirit skills. Rather than meeting the spirit halfway, you are making the spirit come as close to the physical as possible. I have witnessed operations when I could quite clearly sense the spirit, and others could as well, but the Magician kept conjuring and demanding the spirit to appear because he wanted it to be even more visible. This Magician said it's not uncommon for a conjuration to take two or three hours until the spirit was clearly in the crystal. He could sense the spirit's presence just like we could, but to him, the job was not done until something truly paranormal happened. He felt that a spirit was not fully controlled, and therefore not fully safe to talk to, until he could see it in the crystal with ease. That's not how I do things, but it's not an unusual position to take, so I include it here for your information. You choose how to proceed.

POWER AND PASSION

Exorcisms and evocations take a lot of effort. There is not just recitation of calls and conjurations but escalating passions as you repeat your demands again and again. The powers of the God or Gods by which you are invoking the spirit fill you up and spill over as you invoke. Whether your voice gets louder and more passionate or lower and more focused, there is more than just words passing through your lips. You are standing in a pathway of power and becoming part of the machinery of the Gods.

Every new recitation has to be done with more vigor than the last. Once you are so tired that you start to invoke with less and less force, you may as well throw in the towel. It's not happening that night.

Shifting gears from this level of passionate activity to the stillness and receptivity required for clairvoyance can be an almost impossible trick to pull off, yet another reason for the spirit to be pulled as near to the physical as possible. It is also a reason that many Magicians use seers to communicate with the spirit rather than try to do it all themselves.

PARTNERS IN CRIME

John Dee had Edward Kelley. Aleister Crowley had Victor Neuberg. Humphrey Gilbert had John Davis. Jack Parsons had Frater X.[1] Those are just the famous examples. Because it can be difficult to manage the rigors of a conjuration into near physical appearance and still be receptive enough to see the spirit, many texts call for a seer as well as an exorcist. In other words, someone to pass the messages between you and the spirit so that you are free to perform the conjurations and exorcisms.

Apart from having someone dedicated to seeing, there are other advantages to a two-person conjuration. It's as true for conjuration as it is for a hike in the mountains: the buddy system enhances safety. Dangers are real, and in some cases it's not that the spirits are out to get you because they are bad; it's that you are approaching them forcefully in this kind of conjuration and that approach has as many risks as it has rewards. In other cases, yes, the spirit may just like to cause a ruckus or even harm if they can. Sadly, people can be like that too. If the seer starts to display signs of psychic attack, you can exorcise the spirit and shut it down. If the Magician starts to weaken or display signs of attack, the seer can notify the Magician that they may be under attack.

So who do you choose for this kind of work? Traditional texts written a few hundred years ago often call for a young boy to be the seer, much in the way that a Mass calls for altar boys. Suffice to say I think it's a bad idea to bring kids into this kind of ritual no matter what the grimoire says. I will go on record and say that you should never involve kids in this kind of ritual. Please work with adults.

It may be tempting to pick someone who tells you they are very psychically receptive, but you should be careful here as well. Remember the lessons on discernment: someone who sees visions every time they pray is prone to receiving surface-level gobbledygook. That person may not take kindly to putting aside easy visions in favor of deeper probing and tossing things out that are not informative or actionable. My advice is to avoid the people who claim to be wildly psychic and hunt instead for those who are stable and discerning. You don't want to pick someone who is decidedly un-psychic, or who has problems seeing anything, but if you are going to bother with a compelling conjuration that drags a spirit kicking and screaming close to our physical orientation, you don't really need the most psychic person ever. You just need someone who has a similar view to yours, who has a small amount of psychic ability, and who is trustworthy.

Don't skimp on that last quality. The seer is in a position to tell you whatever they want to tell you, and can easily take advantage of that. Edward Kelley told John Dee that the spirits suggested they swap wives. Was that really the Angels or just Edward, who was known to be a somewhat unscrupulous chap to begin with? You should not believe everything a spirit tells you, so if the spirit is speaking through a seer, it is another level of skepticism you should be mindful of.

In the end whether you work with a seer is up to you. I have worked with seers in the past and prefer to work alone. I have, from time to time, had a God or spirit tell me that they wanted to show me a seal that I could not perceive or record on my own, in which case I bring in an artist-seer, such as Matthew Brownlee, who recorded the Lightning Glyphs of Jupiter and planetary seals that I use in my work.

AN EXAMPLE OF A COMPELLING CONJURATION

The tools of the friendly conjuration are basically the same tools you need now with one addition: a symbol of protection to go on the back of the spirit seal. The exact seal you use should correspond to the powers that you are conjuring by. Most classical grimoires are Christian, so the first seal we will use is from that tradition. The reason it goes on the back of the seal of the spirit is to insulate or protect the wearer from the influence of the spirit they are conjuring. The Pentagram of Protection from the *Ars Goetia* has proven well for this conjuration. If doing work in another format, such as a Hekatean conjuration, you want to change the protection seal to something like the Wheel of Hekate.

One clever thing I have seen people do is have a seal of protection made in metal and paint the opposite side with chalkboard paint so that they can draw the seal of any spirit on it. I have also seen seals sold where the protection seal is already on the back of the spirit seal. You can also just wear both seals separately; it is not vital that one be behind the other.

Some people argue that every grimoire represents its own unique system and that the seal of protection from the *Ars Goetia* will be the only seal that is effective on the back of the seal of one of those spirits. Likewise, the circle and other accoutrements would need to be from that book. I disagree, and so does history. As I have already pointed out, the spirit catalogue from the *Ars Goetia* is an evolution of several other books, none of which contain the same diagrams. In Jake Stratton-Kent's groundbreaking work *Geosophia* he noted that in 1535 Benvenuto Cellini and an unnamed Sicilian priest performed several conjurations in the Colosseum in Rome. They brought a stack of books into the circle with them from which to choose conjurations, seals, and dismissals. Yes, the books are written so that you use the materials in that text, but in practice Sorcerers have always been more eclectic.

It's kind of like buying a piece of furniture and the brochure warns you to only use the X-Brand polish and accessories with the piece. You know that any other polish or hardware will work just as well, but they want you to use theirs. I guess what I am saying is that whether it's from this book or a classical grimoire, brand loyalty is not required. Keep that in mind as we progress through the examples of evocations.

Set up the temple the same as the friendly conjuration. You can use a plain circle on the floor, or because this is a compelling conjuration, perhaps you want to set out a more complex circle. You really want to have the seals of the kings on the ground for a compelling conjuration. Or perhaps the names of Archangels and so on.

If you can't or don't want to, it really is okay. It is the demarcation of the boundary and blessing of the circle that makes it active, not the words written on it. The words can add a certain level of manifestation or feeling of "solidity" to the boundary though. Almost like a "no littering" sign in a park: you know you're not allowed to litter and there is a fine if you do it, but the sign is a reminder.

If you use a triangle, or a scrying device for the spirit to manifest in, it should be outside the circle for this kind of operation. To be honest, I almost never use one for this type of work, as I prefer to ask the spirits to simply manifest at the edge of the circle. If you want to use one, then go for it. There are ways to work with a monstrance inside the circle during a compelling conjuration, but for this book, let's just keep it simple: if we are being bossy and compelling spirits to appear with force, let's keep them outside the circle.

As for the ritual to create the circle and keep it, the opening from the friendly conjuration will still hold up. Walk the circle and incense it the exact same way with the same words beginning with "Gyrum Carpo."

Rather than invoking the four kings as you did previously, use this conjuration, which is almost the same but integrates the four Archangels as well.

Face east and wave your wand three times: once to the left, once to the right, and once to the center. Keep your wand pointed at the center and say:

> Oh Raphael, who bound Azael under the desert, guard
> this circle from all danger and harm that comes from
> the East. O Uriens, king most shining, who reigns in
> the East, whose kingdom has had commencement at
> the beginning of the world and which will endure until
> the end of the ages. By the power of almighty God, the

Archangel Raphael, and Saint Cyprian, I humbly yet frankly demand that you open the gates of the East. Let my conjurations echo loudly in the East and your seal serve as a key to your kingdom. Let all spirits who are subject unto your command appear promptly and be subject unto me when called.

Face south and repeat the waving. Point and say:

Oh Michael, leader of God's armies, guard this circle from all danger and harm that comes from the South. O Maymon, king most noble, who reigns in the South, whose kingdom has had commencement at the beginning of the world and which will endure until the end of the ages. By the power of almighty God, the Archangel Michael, and Saint Cyprian, I humbly yet frankly demand that you open the gates of the South. Let my conjurations echo loudly in the South and your seal serve as a key to your kingdom. Let all spirits who are subject unto your command appear promptly and be subject unto me when called.

Face west and repeat the waving. Point and say:

O Gabriel, who razed Sodom to the ground, guard this circle from all danger and harm that comes from the West. O Paymon, king most glorious, who reigns in the West, whose kingdom has had commencement at the beginning of the world and which will endure until the end of the ages. By the power of almighty God, the Archangel Gabriel, and Saint Cyprian, I humbly yet frankly demand that you open the gates of the West. Let my conjurations echo loudly in the West and your seal serve as a key to your kingdom. Let all spirits who are subject unto your command appear promptly and be subject unto me when called.

Face north and repeat the waving. Point and say:

O Uriel, who stands vigilant at the gates of Eden,
guard this circle from all danger and harm that comes
from the North. O Egyn king most strong, who reigns
in the North, whose kingdom has had commencement
at the beginning of the world and which will endure
until the end of the ages. By the power of almighty God,
the Archangel Uriel, and Saint Cyprian, I humbly yet
frankly demand that you open the gates of the North.
Let my conjurations echo loudly in the North and your
seal serve as a key to your kingdom. Let all spirits who
are subject unto your command appear promptly and be
subject unto me when called.

As you can see, the calls are basically the same, but include
the name of an Archangel associated with that quarter. The name
of the Archangel is associated with a deed of either wrath or
guardianship so that all spirits know why their power is invoked.
In the middle of the call, rather than "By the Power of IAO," we
are calling upon "Almighty God" as well as the Archangel of the
direction, and St Cyprian, the saint of Sorcery. Cyprian, as I mentioned earlier, is sympathetic to the needs of Sorcerers and works
well alongside of Archangels when conjuring spirits.

This will set up the circle and get you ready to conjure.

THE PRAYER OF CONJURATION

Focus on the edge of the circle of wherever you hope the spirit to
appear. Pick up your wand and point and say:

Dominus Exercituum, grant us your angels to guard this
circle.
Dominus Exercituum, grant us your seraphim to stand
with flaming swords.

Dominus Exercituum, grant us your power to render
Demons powerless.
Dominus Exercituum, be with us and give us strength.
I, *name*, call, conjure, and compel you, o spirit *name* by all
the Archangels Michael, Raphael, Uriel, and Gabriel,
and by all the choires of thrones, dominations, principalities, powers, virtues, cherubim, seraphim, and all
creatures of God almighty.
By the names Hagios +, Ischiros +, Paraclitus +, Zebaoth
+, Adonai +, Agla +, Athanatos, and by the might
of God the Father +, and by the might of God the
Son +, and by the might of the Holy Spirit +, and
by the words with which Solomon and Manasses and
Cyprian exorcised and evoked the spirits, that you
obey immediately. Appear before me in a comely and
affable form, and answer all that I ask of thee or else I
will damn you forever. Appear peaceably and affably
outside this circle. I command this of you, o spirit, by
the virtue of God the Father +, God the Son +, and
God the Holy Spirit + and by the might by which
everything was created and made. So be it + + +!

This is a shortish compelling evocation. Make the sign of the
cross with your wand every place that there is a cross in the script.
If you are working alone, this is a good place to pause and shift
into a receptive mode and see if you can see or sense the spirit.
Whisper the following while you look.

Prayer of Receptivity

Oh lord of hosts, cleanse my mind with the hyssop of
your grace.
For I stand in the holy of holies of the spirit
Wash from me common understanding of the flesh
And common appearance from my mind's eye

Create in me eyes that I may see with your eyes
What I cannot see with my own
And what I behold, glorifies you in its beholding
Amen

If you don't see anything, that's okay. That's normal, in fact. The trick to evocation is the same trick with exorcism: repeat again and again with escalating passion each time. This is a moment for you to get downright theatric in your performance. Get louder. Get more pointed. Enflame yourself with passion! After a few repetitions you should sound like you are in a movie trying to command a spirit with all the thunder and fury of heaven's host!

If you want to switch it up and go for more violent conjurations, go right ahead. You can look into the grimoires for examples and pull from them. You can also look at exorcisms and switch the wording a bit to command the spirit to appear rather than depart a possessed person. In my Black School program we use conjurations based on the work of Girolamo Menghi, a 16th-century exorcist who was once considered the father of exorcism, but whose books were banned by the church in the early 1700s. He emphasized drawing images of the Demons he was exorcising and using those images in the exorcisms much the way that Magicians would use a spirit's seal.

In general, I tend to stick to one conjuration repeated over and over, no more than nine times. That means that I throw in the towel after about an hour. I should note that some very well-respected Magicians would say that about two hours of conjuration might be necessary, but I have never found it as such. Still, mine is not the only opinion out there and you should be aware of others. Go longer if you feel you want it. As for me, there is no spirit I want to work with *that* badly.

If you want to follow up with a stronger conjuration, or if you are successful in conjuring the spirit but it starts to give you trouble, you can use the following constraint:

Prayer of Constraint

By the names Hagios +, Ischiros +, Paraclitus +, Zebaoth +, Adonai +, Agla +, Athanatos + and by the might of God the Father +, and by the might of God the Son +, and by the might of the Holy Spirit +, and by the words with which Solomon and Manasses and Cyprian exorcised and evoked the spirits, I demand that you obey immediately. As Abraham and Noah obeyed the lord. As Saul obeyed Christ. Even as Jesus was obedient to his parents, so be obedient to me. Cause no disturbance and abstain from all harm, and place yourself calmly before me outside this circle. This I command by the power of God the Father +, God the Son, and God the Holy Spirit.

Prayer of Final Constraint

By the names Hagios +, Ischiros +, Paraclitus +, Zebaoth +, Adonai +, Agla +, Athanatos and by the might of God the Father +, and by the might of God the Son +, and by the might of the Holy Spirit +, and by the words with which Solomon and Manasses and Cyprian exorcised and evoked the spirits, that you obey immediately. Listen and hear, unclean spirit, I admonish and command you by Dominus Exercituum, lord of hosts, that you be barred from heaven and offered no rest in hell. That the Earth itself rejects you and that the air tears you apart. That fire expells you and water rejects you and that no place in this world or others gives you harbor. Place yourself calmly before me outside this circle. Or I shall burn your seal and leave you to your fate. This I command by the power of God the Father +, God the Son, and God the Holy Spirit.

I will be honest: I have never used this or resorted to it. I pride myself on actually doing everything I put into my books, but in this case it's not something I would do. However, I feel like this chapter is incomplete without it. I mean, if you are constraining a spirit with a threat, there has to actually be a penalty, right? Here it is.

DISMISSAL

Whether a spirit has appeared or not, you need to follow this with a dismissal of the spirit. Remember: the spirit may be doing its best to orient itself in a way that you can see it, and you just didn't. This is why I emphasize spirit skills. Even if nothing happened, you disturbed the area enough where you need to dismiss anything that may have been attracted by the rite.

Prayer of Dismissal

By all the Archangels Michael, Raphael, Uriel, and Gabriel, and by all the choires of thrones, dominations, principalities, powers, virtues, cherubim, seraphim, and all creatures of God almighty. By the names Hagios +, Ischiros +, Paraclitus +, Zebaoth +, Adonai +, Agla +, Athanatos and by the might of God the Father +, and by the might of God the Son +, and by the might of the Holy Spirit +, and by the words with which Solomon and Manasses and Cyprian exorcised and evoked the spirits, I now command you to depart from this place and not appear again unless I summon you. As you came in power, go in peace. Amen.

That's it in a nutshell. If this seemed very Christian and churchy, well, it is! That's how this kind of thing was done and I don't see any reason to tone it down or dance around it. You don't necessarily have to be Christian to do this; you simply have to be

Consorting with Spirits

open to it. Much in the way that people are open to engaging in a variety of Pagan paths. If you are not open to it, then don't do it! If you have been traumatized by Christianity or are repelled by it, I totally understand. Don't do this. There are other options.

A HEKATEAN CONJURATION

What would a compelling operation like this look like outside of a Christian context? The first thing to realize is that the names and seals in the grimoires might no longer work or be valid. If you consider the idea that some Magician at some point conjured these spirits and got them to give these seals under conditions like the previous conjurations, then it's worth asking: if the spirit was bound under promises and threats from an Abrahamic God, is it still bound when conjured under a different God?

In general I found the seals to work fine under Hekate's power, but I attribute that more to Hekate's might and longevity than anything else. She was still being written about by Christian Demonologists like Michael Psellos a thousand years after Christ, so her power is enduring. As for any other Gods or Goddesses, I leave that for you to figure out for yourselves through experimentation.

For now, let's take a look at what a Hekatean Compelling Conjuration looks like.

THE CIRCLE

I do not recommend opening with the four kings. No names on the floor, either, just a circle will do nicely, or perhaps a circle with the names of the four rivers and winds within it. Place a triangle outside the circle. No names need to be inscribed there, either. You can place a scrying device in the triangle or a thurible of incense.

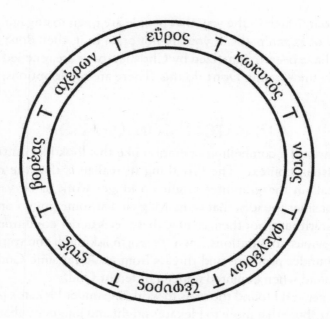

Take a dagger or sword and trace the circle while chanting the following:

> Hekas hekas este bebeloi (away away all ye profane)
> Far, far, be all ye profane.
> From outside this circle burns with the flames of tartarus
> Incinerating any and all obstructing spirits
> Until not even your names remain
> From inside, this circle burns with the torchfire of
>   Hekate
> Illuminating the unseen
> Calling only what has been conjured
> And providing safety to those within.
> By Earth the body of the Goddess
> By Air, her living breath
> By water the pulsing blood of the Goddess
> By fire the burning soul

Consorting with Spirits

By the secret names of Hekate
Aktiophis Ereshkigal Neboutosoaleth
Enoigesan ai pylai tou ouranou!
Open the pylons of the heavens!
Enoigesan ai pylai tes chthonos!
Open the pylons of the earth!
From this point you can move to the center and point to
  the edge of the circle again.

PRAYER OF RECEPTIVITY

Propylaia, throw open the gates of spirit
Phosphoros, illuminate my mind with the light of your
  torches
Propolos, steer me safely through realms of spurur
Physis, bind all Demons in this circle and compel them
  to speak truthfully and without delay.

PRAYER OF COMPELLING

I, *name*, call, conjure, and compel you, o spirit name
In the name of Hekate Chthonia, Queen of Spirits,
To appear at the edge of this circle
In the name of Ereshkigal, Aktiophis, Nebotosoaleth
Appear without delay
Whether you are in the Empyrian heavens, or Hades'
  depths
Or wandering any of the lonely places of this earth.
I stir you and summon you to appear.
In the name of Brimo, Alexeatis, Enodia, Nekuia, Nykte-
  ria, Tartarouchos
And by all the names that Medea and the Witches of
  Thessely commanded the spirits

That you obey immediately. Appear before me in a
    comely and affable form, and answer all that I ask of
    thee or else be hunted forever.
Appear peaceably and affably outside this circle. I com-
    mand this of you, o spirit, by the virtue of the key-
    holder of the worlds

You can repeat this three or nine times, and if you like, you
can construct stronger-worded compelling conjurations, just like
in the previous Abrahamic conjurations. There is no shortage of
epitaphs or names to refer to. If you aren't familiar enough with
Hekate to construct another evocation, then chances are you
shouldn't be forcefully conjuring spirits by her power.

When the spirit appears, ask them your questions or negotiate
an exchange of services for offerings, or whatever other business
you have to conduct. Then give the license to depart.

In the name of Hekate Chthonos, Ereshkigal, Aktiophis,
Nebotosoaleth
    And by all the names that Medea and the Witches of
Thessely commanded the spirits
    I now command you to depart from this place and
not appear again unless I summon you. As you came in
power, go in peace.

Obviously you could arrange other Pagan-based conjurations
using a similar format. You will want to have a circle set up that
makes sense within the context of the Deity you are calling upon,
some sort of directional orientation that aids the appearance of
spirits, a prayer for purification or receptivity, and a group of conjurations that invoke the power of the Deity through names and
deeds.

This really is a place where relationship matters. It may be your
first time encountering the spirit you are conjuring, but it should
not be your first time encountering the powers you are *conjuring them
by*. It is not a matter of your faith or belief doing the work, as some
would believe, but a matter of having spiritual authority built up

within the context you are conjuring under. I have a long history of working in Western magic rooted in Abrahamic religion, and a long history with Hekate, so both of these conjurations work well for me. If I were to decide to conjure a Demon by the power of Odin, I would be on much shakier ground because I have not done any serious work in that field nor built up the relationship to that Deity that I would find reliable.

WHAT ABOUT THE DEVIL?

I gave a Christian conjuration like what you might find in a classical grimoire. I then gave a variation based around Hekate that could serve as a good example for a Pagan conjuration. But what about Lucifer? In the last chapter, I showed how it might look to do a friendly conjuration from a Luciferian perspective, so what would a forced conjuration look like? Would that work? Would it be a good idea?

Many Demonolaters, practitioners who worship Demons religiously, have a taboo against forceful evocations, feeling that they should work exclusively through petition, offering, and prayer and that any attempts to compel Demons go against their spiritual views that are based on consent of spirits. I respect that and sympathize with the view.

That said, if we are talking about the conjuration of Demons, beings that tradition places under the rulership of the hierarchy of hell, then compelling them by infernal powers is going to be a lot different than doing it by the power of YHVH and the Trinity. Rather than a greater power who is opposed to you, the situation is like compelling a lower employee by contacting their manager. We just need to flip it to the infernal side of the coin—if you believe in such a coin to begin with. It is still compelling through force though, and the basic procedure is similar.

Let's start with that circle. The good news is that the seals of the four kings will work well in this context so a simple circle with those four seals will work well.

We can't very well call upon the God or Archangels for conjuring so let's head to this setup:

Gyrum Carpo! (I take/seize the circle!)

Ego (*name*) Consecro et Benedico istum circulum I (I, *name*, consecrate and bless this circle)

.per nomina dei attisimi SATANAS (in the name of the most powerful God SATAN)

Ut sit mihi et omnibus scutum at (That it may be to me and all a shield and)

Protectie fortissimi LUCIFER invicibile (protection in the name of the most powerful invincible Lucifer)

Contra omnes malignos spiritus (Against all malignant spirits)

Eorumque potestates in nomine Satanam Inferi (and powers in the name of Satan and all infernal powers.)

Amen.

Now head in to the conjuration of the four kings.

O Uriens, king most shining, who reigns in the East, whose kingdom has had commencement at the beginning of the world and which will endure until the end of the ages. In the name of Lucifer I humbly yet frankly demand that you open the gates of the East. Let my conjurations echo loudly in the East and your seal serve as a key to your kingdom. Let all spirits who are subject unto your command appear promptly and be subject unto me when called.

Face south and repeat the waving. Point and say:

O Maymon, King most noble, who reigns in the South, whose kingdom has had commencement at the beginning of the world and which will endure until the end of the ages. In the name of Lucifer I humbly yet frankly demand that you open the gates of the South. Let my conjurations echo loudly in the South and your seal serve as a key to your kingdom. Let all spirits who are subject unto your command appear promptly and be subject unto me when called.

Face west and repeat the waving. Point and say:

O Paymon, king most glorious, who reigns in the West, whose kingdom has had commencement at the beginning of the world and which will endure until the end of the ages. In the name of Lucifer I humbly yet frankly demand that you open the gates of the West. Let my conjurations echo loudly in the West and your seal serve as a key to your kingdom. Let all spirits who are subject unto your command appear promptly and be subject unto me when called.

Face north and repeat the waving. Point and say:

O Egyn king most strong, who reigns in the North, whose kingdom has had commencement at the beginning of the world and which will endure until the end of the ages. In the name of Lucifer I humbly yet frankly demand that you open the gates of the North. Let my conjurations echo loudly in the North and your seal serve as a key to your kingdom. Let all spirits who are subject unto your command appear promptly and be subject unto me when called.

A LUCIFERIAN CONJURATION

I, *name,* call, conjure, and compel you, o Spirit X in the name of the son of morning, the Dragon of Lamentation, and the Angel of Exile, I move you with the fire of the first flame.

By the command of your emperor Lucifer, and by all the hierarchy of hell,

By he who is called Wormwood and Prince of the Powers of Air

By he who remains unbowed and who holds the rod of the governance of Earth

I command that you obey immediately. Appear before me in a comely and affable form, and answer all that I ask of thee or else suffer the wrath of he whom you you serve. Appear peaceably and affably outside this circle. I command this of you, o Spirit, by the virtue of Father of the First Flame.

In the name of Lucifer, Baalzebul, Astaroth, and the hierarchy of the fallen.

As with the Hekatean conjuration, you can choose to go further with it if you want to. Go bananas! One could flesh this out with the system of Demons from Abramelin, or the *Grimoire Verum*, or any of the various Theistic Luciferian and Satanic churches. Though I work with Lucifer, I don't really have much of an interest in Luciferianism as a religion, but I feel like it's neglectful to ignore the interests of the growing numbers of practitioners who approach magic through this lens.

TO COMPEL, OR NOT TO COMPEL, THAT IS THE QUESTION

Many of you reading this chapter are probably appalled at the idea of compelling spirits, feeling that it violates the consent of another being. I respect that view, and mostly feel the same way, but you should at least understand the process and have the ability to do it if something were to go wrong with a friendly conjuration or you encounter a local being that decides to stick to you.

Others might feel that the conjurations are too light and that spirits are only safe to interact with when heavily constrained. I disagree, but I respect the view.

Throughout the years I have held a number of different views about what spirits are and how to contact them. I will probably continue to evolve my views throughout the next few decades. Just keep the following rule in mind: *as with people, so with spirits*. Sometimes you will run into situations with people who are aggressive, or destructive, or bothersome, or simply opposed to what you need to get done. In these cases, you will probably need to exercise some level of coercion or compelling to defend yourself or accomplish your goals. You may run into the same thing with spirits. If, however, you try to coerce, influence, and dominate every person you meet, you will hamper your relationships, whereas you otherwise might have enjoyed constructive interactions. It's the same with spirits. Some of the stories of spirits rebelling against conjurors are simply a reaction to being forcibly compelled when simpler and more egalitarian methods would have done.

CHAPTER 10

Intermediary Spirits and Familiars

In the last few chapters, we saw how we can leverage relationships with powerful Deities and spirits to summon other spirits, either through friendly invitation or forceful compelling. There is, however, another method that we should discuss: the use of intermediary spirits. These are spirits who help you contact and consort with other spirits.

Gods and powerful spirits whom you call upon to constrain spirits will carry a lot of weight, but they are also a bit distant and not likely to get directly involved in the operation itself. It's kind of like calling the Amazon helpline and invoking the fact that you know Jeff Bezos. Sure, it will eventually get done, but the name you have called upon is so distant from the poor representative on the phone that it would be better if you had direct access to someone further down the line. If you really knew Jeff Bezos, he would give you a personal concierge to get things done. That's the idea behind an intermediary spirit: you put a significant amount of work in to establish a rock-solid relationship with this one spirit, and it can go out and contact other spirits for you.

In some traditions, access to an intermediary spirit is the mark of spiritual authority. Knowing the names of a Deity is all well and good, but why should anyone listen? If you can call up a powerful spirit directly, one that spirits instantly acknowledge as important, then that is certainly going to help.

The use of the four kings in the last two chapters can function somewhat like intermediary spirits: they open the gateways and establish authority for spirits to listen and take you seriously, but it's still not the same as one single spirit who will intercede for you. Let's take a look at some examples of intermediary spirits in magical tradition.

THE HOLY GUARDIAN ANGEL

The Book of the Sacred Magic of Abramelin the Mage is one of the most famous books of magic in history. Similar to other books, it contains a catalogue of Demons and a selection of magical squares that activate different magical effects, but there is a catch: first you have to attain the knowledge and conversation of your Holy Guardian Angel. This is not just a summoning; it's an intimate connection.

The book prescribes an eighteen-month working during which you pray fervently to God to bring you into contact with your personal Angel who will then act as intermediary. The Angel is an intermediary between you and God, as well as between you and Demons, which get summoned and placed under your power. There have been many variations on this work throughout the years—some do it by the book, but only for six months, which is how the first English translation read. Others do it by the book, but set the time line aside and let it take as long as it takes. Still, others go far off-book and use Aleister Crowley's Liber Samekh as the ritual, but still increase the fervor and time spent on the operation until in the final months it consumes nearly the whole day.

There are some people who place such importance on the Holy Guardian Angel that they claim those who do not possess

Knowledge and Conversation of the Holy Guardian Angel should not be doing magic of any kind. I don't think that is reasonable or accurate, but I can tell you that undertaking the work is a powerful experience. I attained the knowledge and conversation of my Holy Guardian Angel in 1996 after about five months of performing Crowley's Liber Samekh and another four months of performing a stylized rite that is closer to the original version of the ritual from PGM V. Since then, the Holy Guardian Angel has aided me in contacting Gods and spirits that I have been interested in as well as facilitated meetings with people who would help me on my journey.

Any serious discussion of the work requires a book of its own, and there are several available: translations of the original texts, alternative paths advocated by different authors, and diaries of people who underwent the process.

If you decide to do it, I have a few pieces of advice. First, don't listen to people who claim it's advanced work done after many years in magic. Quite the opposite, it's supposed to be done before you do a lot of other work. Second, do it when your life can withstand it. Many people report upheavals during the process, myself included. I did it in my twenties before I had a solid family and career, so it didn't matter much if everything blew up around me. I would never do it now. It's best done in youth or after retirement, in my opinion. Third, don't worry about what people say the Holy Guardian Angel is—do the work and find out.

Often you find people's opinions on this issue evolving over time. For instance, in his early writings Crowley considered the Holy Guardian Angel to be a part of the Self, but later when writing *Magick Without Tears*, he wrote that it was definitely a discrete entity, perhaps a type of being that had passed through our stage of humanity already. I started out thinking it was a part of myself, then was quickly disabused of that notion by the Angel itself.

Of course, the Holy Guardian Angel is not the only type of intermediary spirit.

THE PAREDROS

"Paredros" is a name for a class of helpful familiar spirits that appear many times in the *Greek Magical Papyri*. The nature of the spirit varies according to the Papyri you are reading. Some are powers connected to constellations, some are the spirits of the dead bound into service, and some are simply spirits who are granted by Gods or powers to the Magician. Though I have never done it, the wildest method for obtaining a Paredros in the Papyri involves invoking the Goddess Nephthys. Then, when she tries to leave, you grab her and refuse to let go until she binds the spirit of an old woman into your service by giving you two teeth: one from an ass and one from the old woman.

If you wanted to obtain a Paredros, you could alter the Hekatean invocation from the last chapter so that Hekate makes a Paredros appear in front of you rather than a spirit you already know the name of. I would probably do something less aggressive: I would start by invoking Hekate on a dark moon and making her a large offering of eggs, honey, wine, and incense. Start with one of her classical hymns to link you to the past, followed by the prayer from page 163. Finally, move into your own request for her to grant you a familiar from the hordes of spirits who follow her. She may grant an aoroi (a spirit of the untimely dead) or a Lampad, a night nymph local to the place where you live. There are all manner of Paredroi that the Queen of Witches might grant.

If you want a little help along the way, let me recommend that you do this in the woods at a high place, at a three-way crossroads, or in a graveyard. Etch the seal on the following page on the ground and concentrate on it when you look for your familiar to appear.

SYSTEM-SPECIFIC SPIRITS

Sometimes there might be specifically named intermediary spirits within a given system. Such is the case with Scrilin, the intermediary spirit of the *Grimoire Verum*. The *Verum* is one of the best

and most workable of the classic grimoires and is enjoying a resurgence in popularity mostly due to the work of Jake Stratton-Kent. In that book Scrilin, the emissary of Lucifer, is contacted first so that you can make and consecrate a seal that will summon him. Afterward, you call upon the Arch Demon of your region: Lucifer rules Asia and Europe, Astaroth rules the Americas, and Baalzebul rules Africa. Scrilin will then fetch the various lower spirits for you based upon your needs.

Other systems of magic use different intermediary spirits specific to those workings. In Vodoun, Papa Legba is honored first and opens the gate for other lwa. One of the Books of Saint Cyprian tells how Jonas Sufurino, a monk at the monastery of Brocken, an area renowned for witchcraft, was given two devils in the form of a goat and a dragon that would serve as intermediary spirits for him. These two spirits are still used as intermediaries in some Cyprianic traditions.

SAINTS

If you're Catholic, or have ever picked up a card with a saint on it, chances are you know the phrase Ora pro nobis (*Pray for us*). This is a perfect example of an intermediary spirit. God is pretty far removed from the foibles of human existence, so we appeal to a spirit who is powerful and known to God (sainthood has its privileges), but is also deeply rooted in human struggles and suffering. Sometimes Pagan or Luciferian Magicians wonder why anyone would pray to icons of figures who are crying and suffering rather than displaying power and majesty, but it is precisely their suffering that makes them likely to help!

Of course, saints need not be Catholic. People call upon powerful ancestors as intermediary spirits, as well as Magicians of the past. Padmasambhava, the Sorcerer Saint who brought Buddhism to Tibet, is invoked all the time to summon spirits he once summoned 1,200 years ago and remind them to behave for the Magician.

The devil sometimes gets treated as a saint, even referred to as St. Devil. If you look at it through the lens that Lucifer fell and suffers for a cause of freedom, then he really is a saint. Charles Baudelaire certainly thought so, as you can see in his poem "Litanies of Satan":

> O, Prince of exile to whom wrong has been done,
> who, vanquished, always recovers more strongly,
> O Satan, take pity on my long misery!
> You who know everything, king of the underworld,
> the familiar healer of human distress,
> O Satan, take pity on my long misery!
> You who teach even lepers, accursed pariahs,
> through love itself the taste for Paradise,
> O Satan, take pity on my long misery!

SAINT CYPRIAN

Saint Cyprian is my intermediary spirit of choice for most things. As I am sure you can tell by now, I operate freely in Christian, Luciferian, and Pagan worlds without bias or exclusivity. As a figure that stands between the Christian and Pagan worlds, as surely as he does between heaven and hell, Cyprian is my guy.

My interest in St Cyprian was sparked by a gift: a Peruvian vial amulet given to me by someone who read my book *Protection and Reversal Magick*. Made from what looks like a vaccine vial, the amulet contained a mini horseshoe, red and black huayruro, various pieces of tree bark and vine, Job's tears, and a soapstone statue of St Cyprian. Nowhere is the role of St Cyprian as intermediary made more plain than on the Peruvian Curandero's Mesa, the altar of practice. The Mesa is usually laid out on the ground in a very intricate display of power objects divided into two or more fields. In his book *Eduardo El Curandero, The Words of a Peruvian Healer*, Eduardo Calderon Palomino details the three fields of his Mesa: Campo Justiciero, "The field of the divine judge" on the right; the Campo Ganadero, "The field of Satan or the Sly-Dealer" (here Ganadero or Rancher is an epitaph of Satan) on the left; and the Camp Medio, the mediating field of San Cyprian in the middle. Here, Cyprian is treated as a Christian Saint of Magic who can negotiate between sides on behalf of a Christian Shaman.

On the more Luciferian side, according to the book *Sorcery and Shamanism* by Donald Joralemon and Douglas Sharon, there is a Brujo named Ruperto Navarro operating in Trujillo who made a pact with the devil as a young man. Because of this pact he is forbidden from working with Christ or any of the Christian saints that most Curanderos work with—except for St Cyprian. Navarro's Mesa is divided into three sections in a similar fashion to Eduardo Calderon's with the notable exception that the Ganadero side for harming is on the right and the Curandero side for healing is on the left—the reverse of traditional associations. St Cyprian manages the middle field, where he not only mediates the left and right sides of the Mesa, but acts as the ambassador between Navarro's Diabolism and the Christian world that other Curanderos and most of Navarro's clients operate in.

I am not a Peruvian Shaman, but I can attest to the power of St Cyprian to be an efficient intercessor between the Magician and Angels, or Demons, or any other manner of spirit. In fact, in my own workings, I prefer him to Scrilin when using Demons and seals listed in the *Grimoire Verum.*

FAMILIAR SPIRITS

The title of this book is *Consorting with Spirits* in honor of the crime that Witches were charged with back in the bad old days. Very often the accusation of having familiar spirits was part of those charges and inquisition records are full of Witches describing familiars. Joan Flower and her daughters Margaret and Philippa were accused of Witchcraft back in 1619. Before she was charged, there were stories that she boasted of both Atheism and of consorting with familiar spirits. After she was charged, she claimed, as did many Witches, that their familiars suckled on them like babies, or were fed on blood and milk like pets.

I am sure many women were cajoled to admonitions under torture, but knowing what I know of spirit work, it also would not surprise me to find out that many of these stories were true. Familiar spirits are linked to either the individual Witch or their family. I have met a family in which a familiar spirit has been acknowledged through at least four generations. Now you might get excited at this, thinking that these examples must be the real old-school Pagan Witchcraft people have dreamt of, but in truth every member of that family is Greek Orthodox by religion. A point often overlooked is that a lot of the world's Witchcraft is far more tied up with Christian rather than Pagan survivals. I am not saying that's good or bad, it just is.

By some definitions, having a familiar spirit is the defining feature of Witchcraft. It lives and sleeps alongside you and is intimately connected to you. Where the familiar originates can differ. Some Witches claim that their familiars are ghosts of the dead, nature spirits, Fairies assigned by the Queen of Fairy, or Demons assigned to the Witch by the devil or his emissaries.

Since we spent two chapters discussing Demons in the grimoires, it's important to note that one of the key functions of many Demons in the grimoires is that they grant familiars. So we have a situation where we may spend some time doing a lot of work to contact a famous and well-known spirit so that they can give us a very personalized spirit that will be connected with us, our home, our temple, or however we want to set up the scenario.

The reason that this is such a key thing to understand is that some people feel that any time they need to do magic they need to turn to a spirit from a book. The seals and names of familiar spirits are a hard-won prize to be guarded, and are the key to how a lot of magic is done, both today and in antiquity. It's just that because of the personal nature of familiars, they often don't make it into books.

The good news is that you already know how to get a familiar spirit! Do a conjuration— friendly or forced is up to you—then ask for one!

If you don't want to go that route, then let me recommend my own favorite way of doing it: prayer and offering and silence. Plan for regular practice during a period of time that can last from nine days to nine months. Have offerings and prayer every day several times a day followed by listening and being still so that you can hear and sense the beginning of a spirit introduction. If there is a special place this can be done, then all the better. A room at home is certainly convenient, but a hilltop or lakeside lends a certain level of dedication.

As for the prayer, the secret formula is this: first find some words or liturgy that are linked to history or tradition. Memorize them. They are your anchor and your power. The amp for your guitar or the battery in your flashlight. Somewhere in there, you find space for your own words. Heartfelt words. It's better if you can write them out and think about them and know them ahead of time, rather than just make them up on the spot. You want to repeat them again and again. Then end again with some more traditional words.

There is often a debate in magic between following a formula or making your own spells. I always just shake my head and walk away from these discussions because the answer is: *both*. What you are asking for is a personal spirit, so the rite has to be personal. But you are also asking a power that deserves a level of respect and is not just in your head, so you also want to observe some protocols that will get the spirit's attention and make it feel honored.

MALL SANTAS

Intermediate spirits are not always invoked by the Magician. Often they are invoked by the Deity or other powerful entity to stand in for them. When people receive very direct and involved intercession from a God or Goddess, it is a lower spirit standing in for that divinity. I call this the "mall Santa." Kids stop believing that Santa comes to their specific mall to sit for weeks on end long before they stop believing in Santa at the North Pole. They figure that these guys must be working for Santa. The kids tell mall Santa what they want, and real Santa gets the message. It can be the same with spirits.

Hekate taught me a massive and complex system of magical training throughout the course of fifteen years, but not all of it was taught by Hekate directly. Some parts came through Lampads— night nymphs who acted as her representatives during periods that required a lot of hands-on involvement from the spirit side. There is nothing wrong with this; it happens more than you think.

There is really nothing you need to do. It's just something to be aware of. It keeps the ego in check to know that cosmic Deities are not all up in your business like that.

I take that back. There is something you need to do. You need to be mindful that sometimes a spirit will step into a role you desperately want filled and start playing a part. If you trust that spirit implicitly just because it's a spirit, you might end up in trouble. Even if it is that spirit, you need to use good sense.

In 1998, I spent nearly two days writing apocalyptic predictions that were given to me by a spirit who claimed to be a Senior Angel in John Dee's Enochian system. I don't know if it was or not, but after I collected these writings, the spirit demanded I publish them and make them public. I read them over and asked myself what this really was and why it was good (the same questions I asked you to ask yourselves). I came to the conclusion that the predictions were unlikely, and that whether they were true or not, people having the information would not actually benefit them in any way I could see. It also seemed a little too affected by all the "millennium is coming" hysteria. I deleted it instead of publishing it. Thank goodness I did, because only one of those five predictions came true (three if you really stretch the interpretation).

Just keep the idea in mind. . . . Rather than an ancient Deity you might be talking to a mall Santa.

CHAPTER 11

Relationships and Pacts

"Quick! Pull into that record shop!" I heard the voice as clearly as if it was spoken by a passenger in the car, only there was no one in the seat. It didn't ring in my ears, but it resonated in my head the same way that a physical voice does. In this case, I knew that it was a familiar spirit I had been working with for several years— one that was excellent at finding both people and items that were hard to come by. By 2007 most record stores had already closed their doors. This particular one survived by catering to aging Gen Xers who never let go of comics, toys, CDs, and vinyl. The front windows were blacked out and you had to park and enter through the back. It was like an adult store, but for geeks.

"Now look in the used CDs. . . ." This time the voice was more like an idea that popped into my head, but still with the texture of something not from me. I started combing through the CDs and found something I had spent two years looking for; Kirsty MacColl's "Titanic Days." When I got home, I thanked the spirit, but noted that I had never asked the spirit to find it. In fact, I had not reached out to that spirit in several months beyond including his name in my regular offerings. "Hey, you look out for me, I look out for you" was the answer I received in return.

We've covered what spirits are and how they operate. We've covered different methods of contact and dismissal. We have taken a look at how to find spirits in the local area and how to summon them in different grimoire-inspired styles of conjuration. There is, of course, a lot we haven't talked about. What of planetary spirits? What of Angels? I could keep going and going with different spirit categories and methods, and knowing me, I most likely will in the future. There is something that we need to get to that's more important than all that, though: What do you do once you have a spirit in your life?

Just as it is with people, the "how we met" is interesting, but it's the bits in the middle that matter most. There are no rituals for this and no ways to predict and control everything. At least none that won't cut you off from the good stuff.

Every spirit is different. Every person is different. How Astaroth is with you may turn out very differently than how she is with me. That is the journey. That is the beauty. Unfortunately, it means that I can't really tell you what is going to happen when you start consorting with spirits in earnest because there are too many variables at play.

What I can offer you is some hard-won advice from my own thirty years of practice, as well as advice gleaned from teaching hundreds of students a year in my Sorcery of Hekate and Black School of Cyprian courses. These are the pieces of advice that I find myself relying on in my practice and repeating over and over to students who are doing the work and putting in the time.

DO NOT YIELD SOVEREIGNTY

This is *your* life, so *you* are the one who has to make the decisions. That may sound obvious, but every day I encounter people who want to turn over decisions, and thus responsibility for what happens as a result of those decisions, to anyone *but* themselves. Gods, Gurus, "the universe," and yes, the spirits.

Now, let me say that there is an approach to spirituality that encourages surrendering to the will of God or Gods. You turn your life over to something you invest in that is greater than yourself and trust in the influence of this power. This is not my cup of tea, but it works for some people. It works if you have tested that power and found it reliable, and you have a reliably clear connection to that being or beings. This is rarer than it sounds. It is all well and good to "let Hekate take the wheel," as long as you have a real connection to Hekate that gives useful advice and leads you to a better life. If you don't, then you are really just abdicating responsibility for everything to something that isn't even aware you are doing it.

What usually happens is that people simply start interpreting every good thing in their life as a reward for their faith and devotion, and interpreting every bad thing as "a necessary trial." They will look back and think, "Well if that didn't happen, I wouldn't be where I am, so therefore it must have been *meant* to happen." If that is what you believe, fine. In the religious sense it can be a helpful tool for coping with reality. In such religions there is usually an established code of ethics and teachings you can rely on. It does not strike me as something particularly useful to a Magician, Witch, or Sorcerer. Once you start actively communicating with spirits, it can all turn ugly very fast.

I have seen people take stupid risks with their marriage or their business because a spirit said it was a good idea. I have seen people get into the habit of giving a spirit anything it asked for until they missed rent payments so they could afford to pile altars high with offerings of food and alcohol, which just sat there until it rotted. I have seen people not take good and necessary actions because a spirit told them something might go wrong. When was the last time you did something worthwhile and *something* didn't go a little wrong?

Worse than this is when the spirits are not really the ones giving these messages. People project their own fears, hopes, morality, inertia, and habitual patterns on to the spirits and use it as an excuse to be their worst selves. Maybe that spirit *didn't* tell you to quit your job when you were frustrated. You just quit and interpreted your desire to quit as a prompt from a spirit. Thinking the spirit told you to do it certainly makes the scenario more interesting and shifts responsibility, so we go with that.

There are also those who claim to speak for the spirits. It may be your scryer. It may be your card reader. It may be your favorite occult author. It may even be *you* after you have mastered some of the work in this book. I have seen some good and helpful things communicated by those who spirits speak through. I have also seen some unbelievably manipulative shenanigans go down when people get pressured to turn over money, sex, or service.

The simple rule that can guide you in any of these scenarios is to always ask yourself, "What if a person was telling me this?"

What if this was just ordinary advice that Uncle George told me? Does it still make sense? The answer depends on how much you trust him to be knowledgeable in this field and to not be manipulative in his dealings. You get that through experience.

The bottom line is: Do not let the spirits run your life. Do not let those who speak for the spirits run your life. Maintain your own agency and sovereignty.

Ultimately the decisions you make are yours and the responsibility for dealing with them is yours. Even turning your life and decisions over to a God or spirit like some kind of supernatural BDSM contract is ultimately a decision that *you* are responsible for.

CULTIVATE HEALTHY SKEPTICISM

I am going to repeat something here, but it is something that bears repeating: *there is no such thing as pure unadulterated perception.* It's true for interactions with people and is even truer for interactions with beings that are by definition more subtle.

When you practice something that your experience tells you is real, but which the world says is fake, it can be tempting to rebel by trashing skepticism altogether. This is a mistake. I have met some magic-using folks who seem to believe things simply on the basis that the mainstream says they are *not* true. This is how so many people in New Age and magical communities wind up believing in conspiracy theories. Embrace a healthy skepticism, even of your own experiences.

Better yet, suspend the rush to believe or disbelieve entirely. After you finish with a spiritual experience, tell yourself, "This is what I just experienced." Instead of asking yourself if it's true or not, ask yourself if it's actionable or not. Ask if there is anything new here that you didn't already know, and if there is a way to verify it.

If you conjure Baal and he says that you descended from a 16th-century Witch named Mabel, what do you do with this? Some people I know would instantly adjust their family tree to reflect Mabel and tell their kids and anyone who will listen that they descended from a Witch. Others would junk this idea entirely and assume that they fantasized the whole conversation and forget all about it. What I would do is start researching family history for any sign, and maybe even try to contact Mabel with magic. I might engage with Mabel's spirit if it turned out to be useful, but I would need hard non-magical evidence before I added her to the family tree.

TWISTED LANGUAGE

Apart from our own propensity for projection, some spirits don't communicate as plainly and clearly as we would like. Nature spirits in particular tend more toward a "David Lynch" approach, than a straightforward monologue. If you connect with spirits in a ring of trees near your house and they show you creamed corn and say, "The owls are not what they seem," that is something for you to interpret, not take literally. The Yaminahua Shamans of Peru, who are famous for working with Ayahuasca-induced trances, call this type of spirit language "Tsai Yoshtoyoshto," which literally translates as "language-twisting-twisting."

Susanna Clarke in her novel *Jonathan Strange and Mr. Norrell* noted that humans and Fairies have an inverse relationship regarding reason and magick. Humans have great capacity for the former and less for the latter, whereas Fairies have enormous magickal power but comparatively little capacity for reason.

Anthropologist Graham Townsley interviewed a Yaminahua Shaman about language and spirits who said this: "With my koshuiti I want to see—singing, I carefully examine things—twisted language brings me close but not too close—with normal words I would crash into things—with twisted ones I circle around them—I can see them clearly."

I once asked a nature spirit about a relationship problem I was having, and the answer was an image of a Baked Alaska—not exactly straightforward. So I went and ordered it, and the message became more clear: Baked Alaska is essentially flaming ice cream. We were opposites that combine together to form something delicious, but temporary. Get it?

STREAMLINE AND PERSONALIZE COMMUNICATIONS

One of the myths about Solomonic Magic is that every bit of magic takes a huge ceremonial evocation. It's not true though. You do that large ceremony once for the spirit, maybe a few times if needed. At that ceremony you ask how you can establish easier communication with the spirit, or how to invoke their name in spells without summoning them to full appearance.

Learning this is a game-changer. It's right there in the books, but people tend to ignore it. The idea of establishing new protocols for the spirits is the norm.

What will these be? Well, a combination of what you are able and willing to do, and what the spirit is able and willing to accept is how this shakes out. Just remember rule number one: do not cede your sovereignty.

If Belphegor asks you to offer him a bottle of Talisker 18 (which is around $200) as a weekly libation, you should tell him no. If Maria Padilha asks for a bottle of perfume every week for the rest of your life, you should tell her no. Yet, there are plenty of stories both ancient and modern of people going broke meeting the demands of Gods and spirits who grow ever more demanding in their needs. Most of the time, though, the spirits do not demand as much as we fear, and small offerings of prayers, incense, libations, and occasionally food will more than suffice.

Offerings are a matter of spiritual arbitrage. Astaroth can wield amazing influence over minds and probability, but she cannot actually pour herself a drink or light a stick of incense. Her influence means a lot to you, and your offering means a lot to her.

AVOID ABUSIVE AND PETTY SPIRITS—EVEN GODS

Witches and Magicians: "I will not take blaming, gaslighting, or abusive behavior from anyone! Not my parents, not my lovers, not my boss, not my friends!"

Also Witches and Magicians: "I missed a day of my prayer or offering. How do I appease my Patron God so they don't destroy my life?"

Silly, right? But it happens.

Look, I am not saying that you shouldn't keep commitments you make, but if you get involved in a spiritual relationship where the slightest misstep will cause retribution, you should cut and run because you shouldn't take that kind of abuse from anyone.

Sometimes this isn't happening at all and it's our own projection. "I committed to praying to Jupiter every day and I didn't; now my life is completely falling apart. Help!" Is your life really falling apart because of this? Or is this just the normal amount of negative stuff happening that always happens, but now you can blame someone? If missing a day of prayer is enough for a God to destroy your life, that is not a God worth dealing with.

To be fair, there are spirits who are easily offended, and who lash out at the slightest thing. Just like people, right? But it's not the rule, and it doesn't happen often. When you do come across a spirit like that, fuck 'em. You don't need that grief in your life. If being a Witch or a Magician means living in fear of the spirits you invoke, then you are probably better off being a hedge fund manager or whatever else catches your fancy.

There are times when a spirit is well known as picky and high maintenance. Naga Vases from Tibet, for instance, require a lot of particular care or they will strike back in retribution. A Haitian friend told me a story about a djab his family had that was similarly more trouble than it was worth. When a teacher or tradition tells you, "Hey, this might be more trouble than it's worth," listen to them. It may seem like a mark of dedication to take something like that on, but it gets old real quick.

KEEP YOUR PROMISES

While we should not tolerate petty behavior and extreme punishments for slight infractions, that doesn't mean spirits won't hold you accountable. But just like people do, if you keep breaking your word, they will leave you, and other spirits will be less likely to respond well to your conjurations and petitions, so you should try your best to keep your word.

I will never forget being at a Pagan festival in upstate New York and having a great conversation with Louis Martine about Vodoun. He checked his watch and told me we would have to pick this up later because he was due to give a class. Nothing at this festival was starting on schedule and most speakers were waiting a good fifteen to twenty minutes after their slotted time to start their talk. When I told Louis we would have plenty of time, he said, "Not me. If you want the spirits to respect you, you have to keep your word." He started that lecture on time despite only one other person and me showing up on time for it.

If you promise an offering in exchange for a service, make the offering when the service comes through. If you promise a punishment or withhold offerings if something doesn't happen, you need to keep that promise too.

If you make the commitment to do a practice every day, then you should keep that practice as best you can. That does not mean you can never skip or that you will be perfect. You can tell the difference between trying your best and being lazy or irresponsible with a commitment you made to someone else. You can probably tell the difference when someone breaks a commitment that they made to you. So can the spirits. If you want to have a good relationship, you need to keep up your end of the pact. You can expect a reasonable amount of slack here and there, but that doesn't mean you should push your luck.

REAL BEINGS WILL CHALLENGE YOU

Here is a rule to live by: if the spirit or Deity you are talking to never says no, then you aren't actually talking to one. You are just having a conversation with yourself.

The biggest danger in magic—bigger than spirit obsession or curses—is the potential to just reinforce the status quo you are comfortable with. That job you hate? That crappy apartment? That self-defeating way of thinking? Those excuses that you give yourself? When you use magic or spirits to reinforce and reaffirm those, you are building a cage for yourself. It's comforting and will always assure you that you are okay. But it's still a cage.

EXPRESS YOURSELF IN TERMS THE SPIRIT WILL UNDERSTAND

If you know what drives a person to do what they do, you know how to present arguments to them in a way they will understand. It's the same with spirits and Gods. Let's imagine that you want to increase your income by 30 percent next year. We could just make our prayers or requests or negotiations and say, "This is what I want." That might work. But there is a better way.

If I was petitioning Hekate, I would express it this way:

Oh, Hekate, in order to continue my quest of going ever beyond what and where I am, and becoming ever more as you are, I am endeavoring to increase my income by a third. Sweet Trivia, this will enable me to invest in my travels and learning as well as radiate my actions outward through charity and care.

See what I did there? Hekate's nature, at least as she has presented it to me, is one of always going beyond. Upward, inward, outward, going beyond, beyond. I framed my income request in that light, and got what I asked for.

Now let's petition Lucifer:

Oh, Lucifer, you who refused to bow, help me stand against the forces of poverty and oppression. You who rebelled for pride, help me find my dignity. You who offered Christ the kingdoms of the world, commit again your kindly crime and aid me in increasing my own income.

See the difference? Lucifer's interest is (my opinion) in pride and liberty and rebellion, so we appealed to that nature.

You can do this with literally any Deity or power. How about Venus?

Oh, beauteous one, who spreads charm and influence and love, aid me in increasing my influence in the world. Oh, you who produces the green of plants and magnificence of flowers, help me produce the greenery of wealth and flowering of fortune, that it increases my own attractiveness and charisma.

Get it? Try to frame your requests in a way that will resonate with the spirit you are consorting with and it will pay off.

PREPARE LESS, RISK MORE

When you learned to ride a bike, how many books did you read before trying it? How many relationship books did you read before you asked someone out or went on a date for the first time? Did you learn addition and multiplication by reading about it or by doing it over and over and over?

There are thousands of books about playing chess, but every one of them will tell you that the number-one thing you can do to get better is *play more chess*. Magic is like this. Books, even this one, can only teach you so much. Some things in this book you probably will not even fully understand until you actually risk action. And make no mistake: action is risk. You risk getting off on the wrong foot with a spirit. You risk safety and well-being by opening your life up like this. You risk failure, because sometimes no spirit answers back.

The catch is that non-action is also risk! You risk not ever knowing what would have happened if you just tried. You risk being an armchair occultist who spends more time constructing arguments on Facebook than they do doing magic. You risk not doing the thing that you are so strongly called for, so get on it! No one can do it for you. I teach courses in magic and Sorcery that last months and even years, but if you do not actually risk doing the exercises, you will fail to accomplish, or even comprehend, the later lessons.

Prepare less, risk more. You will get further.

MAKE A PACT WITH A SPIRIT

Written pacts between people and spirits are the basis for many accusations of Witchcraft. In 1634, a literal contract on parchment was introduced as evidence against a priest named Urbain Grandier, who was accused of sexually assaulting a group of Ursuline nuns and causing them to become possessed. The contract is signed by Grandier as well as Satan, Leviatha, Astaroth, and other Demons. It was not the first time accusations of demonic pacts have been made against priests. In fact, it was only twenty-three years before this incident that Louis Gaufridi, a priest of Provence, France, was accused of a pact with Lucifer.

Of course, as with most inquisition trials against priests there was more fiction than fact, and it's doubtful that either of these priests made an actual pact with Demons. Torture-based confessions and manufactured evidence be damned. That said, pacts with spirits are a thing.

If you pray and you ask a Deity for help and promise something in return when you get it, you just made a pact with a spirit. If you are out contacting a spirit of the land where you live, or through a friendly conjuration, and you ask for something in exchange for something, you just made an even better pact with a spirit because they had input into the contract. It does not matter that it's not written down. It's still a pact.

If you do decide to write a pact, it can actually be quite a powerful talisman or altar piece as well as a channel for you to continue to communicate with the spirit. Let's get something out of the way right here: as cool as it would be to conjure a spirit into such corporeal manifestation that it could lift a pen and sign its own name, I have never been able to do so. Instead, you speak to the spirit and get their permission to make their seal, or if you are talented with automatic writing, ask them to take over your hand and sign the paper.

What do you ask for in a pact? The same kinds of things you would ordinarily shoot for with magic: something that is within the realm of possibility, but something that is still difficult to achieve. For more information on magical goal-setting, see my book *The Elements of Spellcrafting*. Everything I said in that book about magical goals applies here as well.

What do you give in exchange? Thankfully, *not* your soul. I have made pacts with spirits during which I made offerings to a lodestone that was set upon their seal every day for a year, then buried the stone in a particular place. I have made pacts to leave offerings on street corners or crossroads in exchange for a single act of service. I have made pacts to give to the poor in the name of some spirits, and to anoint the statues with oil to others. I have made pacts to commission artistic representations of spirits. I have even made pacts to dedicate books I have written.

Once you have a written pact, seal it with wax and keep it somewhere safe and sacred. Keep up your end of the bargain but watch and make sure the spirit keeps their end of the bargain as well. If you make a pact to get promoted to a director position within a year, and a year passes and you are still in the same spot, you owe that spirit nothing. Tear up the pact and burn it.

This whole chapter has been about pacts. If you don't have a grasp on the relationship advice and magical advice that I gave, then your pacts might not work out well for you. Contact and conjuring are the easy bits. Consorting and carrying on are the parts that take more work.

CHAPTER 12

Questions and Answers

In some of my courses I give lengthy Q&A sessions between the lessons. A lot of students tell me that those Q&As are what make the class and wind up giving as many poignant moments of useful instruction as the lessons themselves.

When I was deciding how to wrap up this book, I thought a Q&A might be the way to go. I sent word out to about 1,000 students that I wanted their questions on spirits. Obviously, I cannot include them all here, so I am choosing a few of my favorites.

What is the trick to discern spirit communications from ego?
Meditate regularly so that you know the texture and content of your own mind so intimately that you can easily discern outside input. Beyond that, be wary of communications that blow up your ego and make you feel special. The community is filled with people who are "chosen by the gods" but who can't seem to manage even the basics of life that most people can.

How important is it to have a name from a spirit?
It can be important in some contexts like conjuration, but in the end there are work-arounds. Magicians call upon spirits they don't know the name of all the time: "Spirit of this Lake . . ." and so on.

After you make contact, you can work on getting the name to make communication easier. I once called upon "Spirits who have been attached to me since birth" to startlingly good effect.

It's important to remember that even names of Gods and Angels are almost always something humans ascribed in history. We have the power of naming and all that.

What would prevent a spirit from lying?

There are various commands and names that are said to force spirits to tell the truth, but you know what? We have no way of really knowing if they work. I prefer to think of it in the same way I do with people. How do we know when people are lying?

Is there a motive to lie? Is what they are saying unlikely to be true? What other ways can I confirm or refute what has been said? Eventually it comes down to relationships that you trust based on consistent quality of information and action.

In the show *Mad Men*, Don Draper wasn't really Don Draper, but he made a better advertising exec than the real one would have. Who cares what his real name was?

What is the most dramatic, unexplainable, mind-blowing encounter you've had with a spirit?

Possibly the one exorcism that I utterly failed to pull off. I was young and relied too much on Lesser Banishing Ritual of the Pentagram type stuff. Lights were flicking on and off and cabinets were opening on their own. I spiked a fever and took refuge at a Shrine of Perpetual Help. The people in the house moved shortly thereafter.

There have been other encounters with bombastic phenomena, but that one came to mind.

What are some indicators that your relationship with a spirit has become toxic or obsessive? That is, when is it time to move on?

The same ones that happen with people. They are making demands that you do not wish to meet and turn threatening when you don't meet them. They are intrusive and jealous. They punish for small infractions, and so on.

Why do spirits rarely manifest in a super obvious way?
For the same reason that you don't make a big splash in the Astral World. They are not oriented to the physical level and you are.

I cannot see them at all. I am spiritually blind though I have had success working with them. Any tips on how to work on my "senses"?
Use the spirits skills in the book, but to encapsulate it even further, follow these pieces of advice in order:

When something happens, anything at all, follow it without judgment. Engage the fantasy. Debunk yourself *after* it happens. If you question a spiritual experience while it is happening, it won't happen because you are literally disengaging the parts of the mind required to let it happen.

Meditate and cultivate stillness. Seriously, just sit and do nothing. The ability to sit and listen is something we are all losing.

Follow your physical senses and how they work with your mind. Your eyes pick up light and your ears pick up sound, but it's your mind that takes that and creates a meaningful experience. If you follow that process with your mind, you can follow it back out and pick up on other sources of input.

Inner Heat Practice. I cover this in *Sex, Sorcery, and Spirit.* The practice is difficult, but it's not *that* difficult. The payoff is huge.

Are there any failproof ways to communicate with spirits?
As far as I have been able to tell, there are no failproof ways to
do much of anything. Something as subtle as communicating
with spirits is bound to fail sometimes. People who never fail to
communicate with their spirit of choice have likely never actually
communicated with anything other than their own fantasy.

Why do spirits want to help us?
Why not? You give offerings that they find enjoyable and they
help. You command them or threaten them and they help. Sometimes you just ask and they help because they are not pricks. Then
again, sometimes they don't.

**What do you do when you feel like you're not being heard
by the spirits?**
There are always three things at play: you, the mode of communication you are using, and the spirit.

Start with you. How are your skills? How strong is your spiritual authority? If improving that doesn't work, look at the mode
of communication. Maybe seances are not what you need. Maybe
evocations are not what you need. There are so many ways to
reach out, so try something different.

Finally, if it's simply that the spirit doesn't want to listen or
communicate, you either resort to compelling methods or you
decide it's not worth it and find a different spirit.

**Apart from offerings, how can I deepen my connection with
them? How do I attract more spirits to me?**
You deepen relationships with spirits the same way you deepen
connection with people: through repeated offerings, practice, and
communication. I love to write books, but I spend most of my
teaching effort on courses, specifically because people need to
be taught long-form methods of deepening and discerning their
communications.

Attracting more spirits is different. Increase your offerings and
competency at magic. This increased spiritual authority, as well

as the opening of offerings, will start to attract spirits. Rituals like Winds and Rivers or any kind of directional invocation will also orient you to pulling in spirits.

We distinguish one human from another because we have bodies that provide clean boundaries between us in physical space; I am here, and you are there, and there is space between us. What does it mean to distinguish between non-embodied things, or things that don't exist in a physical space? How do you do it?

It works differently at different levels. Ghosts and some nature spirits have a very etheric orientation in that they manifest somewhere specific in space. You can point to them in a room when they are present. Other beings oriented to more subtle levels are harder, and it's more like discerning voices in a room. It's a frequency thing rather than a space thing.

Higher up the chain of subtlety, it becomes impossible to speak in these terms because it's more like code than anything else. It is all there, but we can still interact with parts of it. This is why mystics wax poetic about their experiences and how inseparable they are from what they experience. As Meister Eckhart said: "The eye through which I see God is the same eye through which God sees me; my eye and God's eye are one eye, one seeing, one knowing, one love."

How do you tame the fear that arises when spirits make contact? I often find that I panic and either do something rude (and deal with the consequences) or pull myself away from the experience.

I watch fewer horror movies. That's not a joke. People have become programmed to think that their magic is effective enough to get them into trouble, but not enough to get them out. Avoid horror-movie thinking.

The other technique is to feel the excitement underlying the fear. Latch on to that. Once you get a feel for that, the fear turns into an "I'm about to bungee jump" kind of fear.

Finally, do a stoic exercise. Play out the worst-case scenario from doing X, and determine how likely that is to happen. Then spend the same amount of effort playing out what happens if you do *not* do X out of fear. Most of the time you will find that the danger or loss from not trying outweighs the potential loss from doing it.

Do you attract or repel a different class of spirits throughout your lifetime? If so, is it due to your own growth?
We do often attract and repel spirits that are akin to our nature. There is nothing mysterious about this, as we do it with people too. If you like to get shit-faced and violent on the weekends, then you are going to attract people and spirits who dig getting shit-faced and violent. If you like to set goals and achieve them, then you are going to attract people and spirits who appreciate that. If you like to sit around and philosophize, then you attract spirits and people who love that.

Magic is oriented toward humans seeking help from spirits. Is there any circumstance when it's the other way around?
When you get involved with spirits regularly, there are oodles of examples of this working the other way around. The problem is that people read books, and more books, and even more books and do comparatively little practice. This means that the processes of magic that are topics in these books get more attention than the actual experience of Magicians.

Aaron Leitch recently wrote a piece on how Solomonic Magic is not all about evoking. He is right, but people like books and the books are filled with the process rather than what results from the process.

When you've spent decades refusing to perceive a class of spirits (for example, ancestors), how do you go about removing the shield you built to shut them out?

You just have to decide you want to reach out and do it. You built the wall, and there is nothing more to tearing it down than taking it down one brick at a time.

Of course, sometimes we build a wall for a reason. As more people in the general occult community also become initiated into African Traditional Religions, there can be a pressure to relate strongly with the ancestors because that is the bedrock of most of those traditions. I think that's a good thing in general, but not for everyone and not the universal way to do magic. Some people have a very hard time dealing with the sins of their ancestors. Other people might hold trauma from the religions of their birth, which eventually led them to seek magic or Witchcraft in the first place. No one is understanding orders to get right with their ancestors or spirits of a religion that they are traumatized by. It can be a rewarding thing to undertake, but there are plenty of other rewarding things to do in life, and you can't do them all.

How do we know what not to do when it comes to spirits if there are no indicators of possible offenses?
How do you know what not to do with people if there are no indicators of possible offenses? The tactics are the same. You do a reasonable amount of research and then you do what you think is polite and respectful based on that. If they point out a way that you are being offensive, you adjust course. If they get outraged at slight offenses made in earnest, then you walk away because they are acting in bad faith and who needs that shit?

How do you know you have invoked or evoked a particular spirit? Are there questions you ask them about their identity?
My advice is to trust that they are who they say they are and judge them from the quality of the information or actions they give.

Don't get me wrong. I know that there are procedures for throwing names and threats at a spirit to make *sure* it tells the truth, but honestly it's obnoxious.

Imagine the following scenario of us meeting at a conference:

"Hi, are you Jason Miller?"

"Yes, I am. Nice to meet you!"

"Are you really? How do I know?"

"Uhhhh, you called me, and I answered, and I am telling you I am."

"Well, just to be sure I am going to cage you in this triangular cage and *demand that you tell me the truth!"*

"I am telling you the truth, and I am going to kick your ass when I get out of this cage."

"By the power of Arceus the Creator I demand that you tell me your true name!"

"Uhhhh . . . Jason. Miller."

"Okay, now that's settled. Would you kindly do some magic to help me get a girlfriend?"

That all seems really silly, but it's pretty much what some Magicians suggest you do.

Does the past-life model and reincarnation concept conflict with the ancestor model? Can someone be reincarnated and also function as an ancestor at the same time?
We are more than just one thing. The idea that we are just a body and a spirit is fairly new. Most religions can break down the Self into various parts. I don't want to get into all the specifics, but we can say that part of us reincarnates, part can become an ancestor, part can be a ghost that stays behind, and part is beyond all this.

If a spirit wants to take you somewhere with them, how do you know when not to go? There are places I've been asked to go to, like into a cave or through a portal, that make me feel hesitant. I had one experience where I went and felt like I shouldn't have trusted the spirit to take me there.
You know it the same way you know not to get into the white van with the shady-looking dude offering you candy. It feels sketchy.

Fear can come from excitement, like skydiving or spelunking, but fear can also be from people and spirits who skeeve you out or want something from you that's not in alignment with what you are willing to give.

Hold your ground. The number of people willing to accept crap from spirits that they would never accept from humans always shocks me.

If I get a hunch or a brilliant idea, how can I know whether it was just me coming to a conclusion or was I being spirit led? And if I was being spirit led, how can I know whether it was my ancestors, guides, or my Deity communicating with me?

If you got a hunch or a brilliant idea, then count it as yours, or perhaps a product of your eudeimos, your genius. If you did prayers or conjured for it, then you can attribute it partly to the beings you petitioned, but it's still working through you. A better question is: why is it important to parse this information? Think of it as a combination of all the above.

Is there any technique to induce one of those "can't put the toothpaste back into the tube" moments with a spirit? You know, where it manifests physically, or there is such a synchronicity as to leave no doubt of its existence?

Do lots of magic and two things will happen: 1) You will have a few of those paranormal supernatural moments that cannot be explained eventually; and 2) you will get results that are more subtle, but still giving you what you sought. When you get these consistently over time, the sheer number of them becomes impossible to explain away.

There is no way of inducing the paranormal or miraculous for sure every time, and in the end, while those occasional "knock-your-socks-off" experiences are awesome, it's the consistent small wins that are more useful.

Are different experiences/interpretations of the "same" Deity merely different facets of the whole of its nature, or are they different spirits?
Think about people. The person my kids know me as is quite different from the person you know me as. When I had a day job, the people I worked with knew me as something different than either of those. If someone crosses me seriously, they know yet another Jason: one who doesn't often get to come out and play.

If people can be this varied in how they manifest, how much more varied are subtle beings? Given the subtle nature of the communications, and of the people communicating, it's amazing that the commonalities that exist are as strong as they are.

What are your thoughts about the often "incidental" connections to spirits we create through spellwork, and would you give some pointers to make connections with spirits or certain spells to enhance them?
People who master Astral Projection or types of Spirit Vision and communication can go to a subway stop and seem to be sitting silently while actually making offerings and communicating. There is a lot that can happen at that level. We didn't touch much on this in the book, but doing magic "in the spirit" happens.

Sometimes it can also be amazing to ask a spirit during a spell to do something and show you how they do it. You can learn so much that really cannot be explained easily in books this way. Half the magic I do comes from this type of exploration and only maybe 30 percent of that can be explained in books and courses.

Other than evocation, is there a simple way to quickly "tune in" to the resonance of a spirit's aspects along any of the levels?
You have to have some kind of first contact first. Evocation is one method. Extensive devotion until contact is made is another. Traveling to sacred places or spirit locations is another.

There is no way to quickly tune in to anything, anywhere, anytime. There are people who *claim* you can, but I have not been impressed with anything such contact produces. That said, to each their own.

What is your opinion about working with spirits versus working solely with one's own higher self or Holy Guardian Angel?

I reject the premise. There is no conflict here like you can only do one and not the other. Doing one will actually help you do the other.

At what point do thought forms cross the threshold from being a highly developed thought form into becoming their own sentient, independently functioning "spirit" (so to speak)?

I believe that most thought forms are inhabited by formless spirits anyway, so when you create a servitor or an "artificial spirit," you are just birthing and giving form to a spirit. I have written about this elsewhere, but there isn't room for a full treatment of servitors in this book.

Can a spirit be more than one place at a time?

Some can, some can't. It depends on their level of orientation. A very etheric manifestation of a Ghost or Hill spirit might not, but an Archangel can with no problems.

What is the best way to handle destructive, malicious spirits?

Not bothering with them at all.
   Exorcising them so they are under your control.
   Walk softly and carry a big wand.

Starting out in my magickal youth, I was told that blood is spiritual currency and that it should always be offered.

Now I know more and don't regret giving blood to certain spirits, but does blood bind you to a spirit?

Offering your own blood doesn't irreparably bind you to a spirit, no. There is more poppycock that people talk about with blood and spirits than I can deal with here.

People get attracted to the idea because it sounds "dark" or hardcore. Let me just say that it's neither. If you have ever been to a religious ritual where animals are traditionally sacrificed, there is nothing dark about it, anymore than there is something dark going on when you kill a chicken for dinner. I don't sacrifice animals in my practice, but I have attended both Vodou and Hindu ceremonies where animals were killed in offering. They are community affairs, not dark magic. I would not recommend offering your own blood unless you had a very solid reason for it.

Have you ever had an experience with a spirit you thought was benevolent but actually turned out to be malevolent? Or vice versa?

Yes. Both, in fact. Just like with people, you cut ties in the first case and make amends and build bridges in the second. I had one spirit who was connected traditionally with bats. As soon as I started working with him, a bat flew into the house. I asked that it never happen again. It happened again. That's not really malevolence, but more of a pain in the ass than I am willing to deal with. I no longer work with that spirit.

Azmodeus gave me the impression he wanted to kill me twenty years ago, but that turned out to be the mode of contact I was using. So there ya go.

What are spirits doing when they aren't interacting with humans?

Some are interacting with other spirits. Some are interacting with us without us knowing. Some are like The Dude. They abide.

What about living humans as spirits? In what way does our spiritual nature resemble that of other kinds of spirit, and in what way is it different?
Yes! We are spirits who have the advantage of a body, but the disadvantage that comes with that as well. Still, we can do a lot of the things people believe can only be done by non-corporeal spirits.

Is there a way to get clearer on what is legitimate information? I've had information come through that is not necessarily actionable but is pretty far out and abstract. Is this something that will possibly be understood further down the line or just white noise?
When the information is abstract or mystical, it may not be actionable or testable in any fashion. I love stuff that relates to creation, the nature of the universe, and states of mind. It's the sort of thing that I hope to spend my last days mulling over and contemplating. When I get this stuff, I just take it as is and consider it a point of data. I don't need to come to a firm conclusion.

It's not something I deem true or untrue; it's something a spirit said that I may or may not find useful. If it becomes useful one day, and it's amazing how sometimes abstract mystical stuff can become the basis of something profoundly useful, then it gets tested and proven. If so, just make a note and file it along with all the other things we are not sure of, like what nature or God is, or whether milk is healthy or not.

What are some common misconceptions about spirits?
Oh, *so many.*

- That they are inherently good and truthful.

- That they are inherently evil and untruthful.

- That they are parts of our mind.

- That they have nothing to do with our minds whatsoever.

- That you must never ever contact spirits outside your culture.

- That you can just contact anything from any tradition in any way you want.

Is it true that if you demand true identity of a spirit it can only tell the truth?
It's mostly wishful thinking. Even if they tell you that it's accurate, that might just be a clever cover for a lie.

Consorting with Spirits

What is the difference between a Deity and a spirit?
A Deity is a bit larger than a spirit. They can manifest as a spirit, but that manifestation is just a manifestation of something bigger.

Is there a chance when doing pendulum work or a Ouija board that you are interacting with a spirit? Most say you are connecting with your higher Self. If so, can they be malevolent/baneful?
There is a chance that it's a spirit you are interacting with, but it's unlikely that they are malevolent and baneful. I don't know why people feel that evil spirits are lurking behind every Ouija board but they really aren't.

Why does spirit magic work? Or, I guess more bluntly: why the heck do they take the jobs we give them? Light, booze, and incense seem sore payment for big working like a life overhaul and political magic, and yet it works. So what gives?
Well, what that means to them is something different than what it means to us. I have a student in Argentina I gave several courses to in exchange for a few items that I am sure cost less than $100 (I hope). Their value to me, however, was immense because I can't get them here in the States! I made out like a bandit and so did he. This is how it can work with spirits. That's why I call it spiritual arbitrage.

There is a saying: "No magic without spirits," implying that every magical action is necessarily carried by a spirit. Is it possible to do magic without spirits?
Excuse my language but this saying is bullshit. Yes there is magic that you can do without spirits, because you are a spirit. People have been doing magic with their own minds and bodies since the dawn of time. How do they think we even get the attention of spirits if not through magic?

A lot of your teachings seem to come from "ongoing revelation" as opposed to traditions. When working with spirits, is it best to stick with the traditional route? Or is it okay to experiment?

All traditions are ultimately from ongoing revelations. It's absolutely great to experiment and to root your experimentation in tradition and research. Revelation and research are like two hands that can work together and also two forces that can check each other when focus on one overshadows the other.

When looking at various traditions, particularly closed versus open traditions, how does it apply to the spirit realm? Is the spirit realm universal and just recognized under different names based on tradition? Or are there specific spirits connected to specific traditions that are not to be interacted with unless you come from said tradition?

Oh man, that's quite a question. The answer is simply: yes.

Yes, there are open traditions and closed.

Yes, some that claim to be closed can be opened from outside.

Yes, that some are really closed no matter what.

Yes, that aspects of some spirits are universal.

Yes, that the spirits themselves are still different.

So yes, it's a big, messy, complex, world out there. Bigger than what we know, and bigger than what we *can* know.

And it's *filled* with spirits.

Parting Words

There is a lot more that I could put into this book. We could talk about how you evoke a Planetary Spirit under the power of the Planetary Intelligence, and arrange the temple according to those correspondences. We could talk about how to use a human skull as a vessel for the dead to communicate through. We could talk about the different types of spirit houses, and what it means to have one as a home for spirits to inhabit freely versus one that is bound to a vessel against its will. The list is as endless as the magical art itself, and unfortunately the publisher gave me a deadline and max word count, so I have to stop somewhere.

I hope you realize this book is more than just some invocations, spells, and ceremonies to add to your occult collection. Those bits are here, but what I wanted to give you is something that not many other books have done: give solid advice for how to navigate a life filled with spirits.

I read somewhere once that people think in terms of Head, Heart, or Hand. The Head wants to know what something is. The Heart wants to know what something means. The Hand wants to know how something is useful. If you have read this book, you know that I am primarily concerned about the Hand.

When it comes to magic and spirits, the theories and conjectures about the way things are and are not all leave me unimpressed, and so I have only included theories of how things are to the degree that they prove useful. I live with the expectation that in ten years I will think differently than I do now, and in 100 years people will hold ideas that I can not even conceive of now.

What spirits and Gods mean is something that must be experienced by you. From interactions with lower spirits that seem almost like conversations with another person, to world-shaking mystical experiences that change the course of your whole life, reading about them can inspire, but ultimately I am more interested in you having these experiences than I am in you reading about mine.

I am a person of the Hand. I want to know how something is used, what it does, and why that thing is good. I hope that this book is something that you can take up in your hands, and that I have shown how it can be useful, and why it's good to use it.

Thank you for reading.

Jason Miller
Candlemas, 2021, Vermont.

Notes

Chapter 1
1. *www.merriam-webster.com*
2. *www.forbes.com*

Chapter 2
1. I was using the term "mirror realm" for ten years before the Doctor Strange movie came out. I am not saying they got it from me, but I am not going to stop using the term just because it's in a movie.
2. Alfred Korzybski, *Science and Sanity,* p. 58.
3. Joseph Peterson. *The Secrets of Solomon.* CreateSpace Independent Publishing Platform. (May 26, 2018).
4. It is exactly nine days between the feast of St Cyprian of Carthage and St Cyprian of Antioch—a period that is known as "the Days of the Cyprians."

Chapter 4
1. *www.nbcnews.com.* The bowl is inscribed DIA CHRSTOU O GOISTAIS (By Christ the Sorcerer).

Chapter 6

1. Irish stores usually carry blackthorn items that you can repurpose.

Chapter 8

1. *Necromancy in the Medici Library*. An Edition and Translation of Excerpts from Biblioteca Medicea Laurenziana, MS Plut. 89 sup. 38 Hadean Press Limited (March 30, 2021)
2. I say "her" because this is how Astaroth has always appeared to me and links to her origins. Clearly Astaroth is treated as a "he" in the books in question.

Chapter 9

1. There was a magical partnership between Jack Parsons and L. Ron Hubbard, but we can't be sure that he was a seer. That is, however, what I have been told.

Also by Jason Miller

Protection and Reversal Magick

Financial Sorcery

The Sorcerer's Secrets

The Elements of Spellcrafting

Sex, Sorcery, and Spirit

About the Author

Jason Miller has devoted thirty years to studying practical magic in its many forms. This is his sixth book. He runs multiple online training courses designed to immerse students in deeper and more comprehensive systems that cannot be taught in books.

He has belonged to a few groups, traveled to a few magical places, and been initiated into this and that, none of which are very important. What is important is that he can do magic that actually works and is told he can teach other people how to do that magic in plain language. He hates writing about himself in the third person.

He lives in the mountains of Vermont with his wife, two children, cat, and company of spirits.

Find out more at *www.strategicsorcery.net/*.

About the Illustrator

Matthew Brownlee is an occultist, martial arts teacher, flaneur, and visual artist located in Media, Pennsylvania. He is a graduate of the Philadelphia Art Institute and works at Baker Street Tattoo in Media, Pennsylvania. He is currently working on an oracle deck of spirits and seals.

Visit him at *www.bakerstreettattoo.com/*

To Our Readers